KING LEAR

AF622246

WILLIAM SHAKESPEARE

With an Introduction by

M.K. Bhatnagar
Formerly Professor, Department of English,
M.D. University, Rohtak

PEACOCK BOOKS

Published by
PEACOCK BOOKS
7/22, Ansari Road, Darya Ganj, New Delhi-110002
Phones : +91-11-40775252, 40775214, 23273880, 23275880
Fax : +91-11-23285873
Web : www.atlanticbooks.com
E-mail : orders@atlanticbooks.com

Peacock Books is an imprint of
Atlantic Publishers and Distributors (P) Ltd

First published 1608
Editorial and Design Copyright © Peacock Books, 2023

All rights reserved. No part of this publication may be reproduced, stored in a retrieval system, transmitted or utilized in any form or by any means, electronic, mechanical, photocopying, recording or otherwise, without the prior permission of the copyright owner. Application for such permission should be addressed to the publisher.
All disputes are subject to the jurisdiction of Delhi court only.
Printed & bound in India by Atlantic Print Services

CONTENTS

CONTENTS

SHAKESPEARE'S PLAYS WITH THEIR PROBABLE APPROXIMATE DATES

There is absence of total agreement on the dates of Shakespearean plays. Some scholars give an earlier date than the one suggested here for Shakespeare's first play. Doubt also remains concerning the actual order of composition in particular years. Having stated that, the approximate dates are given hereunder, as largely accepted by Shakespeare scholars in general.

1590-91
Henry VI Part II
Henry VI Part III

1591-92
Henry VI Part I

1592-93
Richard III
Comedy of Errors

1593-94
Titus Andronicus
Taming of the Shrew

1594-95
Two Gentlemen of Verona
Love's Labour's Lost
Romeo and Juliet

1595-96
Richard II
Midsummer Night's Dream

1596-97
King John
Merchant of Venice

1597-98
Henry IV Part I
Henry IV Part II

1598-99
Much Ado About Nothing
Henry V

1599-1600
Julius Caesar
As You Like It
Twelfth Night

1600-1601
Hamlet
Merry Wives of Windsor

1601-02
Troilus and Cressida

1602-03
All's Well That Ends Well

1604-05
Measure for Measure
Othello

1605-06
King Lear
Macbeth

1606-07
Antony and Cleopatra

1607-08
Coriolanus
Timon of Athens

1608-09
Pericles

1609-10
Cymbeline

1610-11
Winter's Tale

1611-12
The Tempest

1612-13
Henry VIII
Two Noble Kinsmen

WILLIAM SHAKESPEARE

BIOGRAPHICAL SKETCH

1. A Symbol of Culture

Introducing Shakespeare to the general reader, G.B. Harrison begins his book with the following statement:

> No household in the English-speaking world is properly furnished unless it contains copies of the *Holy Bible* and of *The Works of William Shakespeare*. It is not always thought necessary that these books should be read in maturer years, but they must be present as symbols of Religion and Culture.

Not only in the English-speaking world, but everywhere, acquaintance with Shakespeare's plays is regarded as a mark of culture; and there is hardly any language-community in the civilized world, which does not possess Shakespeare in translation.

2. Life

Anyone looking for reliable historical information about Shakespeare is bound to meet with disappointment. We get very little help from his contemporaries in the form of recorded reference allusion, or memoirs, Shakespeare himself is completely silent about himself, and as regards his works, he has consumed himself into them so perfectly that it is very risky to draw any clear inferences from his works—except, perhaps, the sonnets, some of which, departing from the convention, appear to be expressing personal experience. We do, however, get some definite information from the parish register, legal documents and town records.

At first sight, it may appear astonishing that such a great writer as Shakespeare should have received no notice from his contemporaries and that no attempt should have been made to preserve every bit of the records associated with his life. But a second look at the state of affairs and attitude to biography prevailing in that period will mollify our uneasiness. The Elizabethans, generally, were indifferent to biographical and autobiographical notes and memoirs; even the biography of the most important personage, Queen Elizabeth herself, is full of gaps and guesses. It should, in fact, be gratifying that we possess more of authentic information about Shakespeare than about any of his contemporary writers excepting Ben Jonson. Moreover, Shakespeare, until very late in his life, was a very ordinary individual belonging to the socially unwelcome profession of actor; and the playwrights, too, were not much distinguished in the society. The critical response to his work was not unmixed high praise until the end of the eighteenth century. It was only in the beginning of the nineteenth century that Shakespeare became established as a great writer who must be spoken of with a feeling of reverence. But during the intervening centuries, he had been steadily moving towards the highest position, and as this process advanced, his admirers became over enthusiastic to complete his biography. The result was an infusion of a great deal of guesswork aggrandisement and romanticising. In such a situation, the best policy will be to keep close to the attested facts and reasonable inferences, except in cases where a highly dubious anecdote may, nevertheless, indicate some important turn in the dramatist's life.

William Shakespeare—the surname is found spelled in various other ways, which was not unusual in those days—was the son of John Shakespeare of Stratford-on-Avon. In 1556 John Shakespeare bought a house in Henley Street. In 1552, he, along with two neighbours, had been fined for keeping an unauthorized dunghill on Henley Street, which means he had been dwelling there for some years before he bought the house. In 1557 he married Mary Arden, the daughter of Robert

Arden, a land-owning farmer who lived in Wilmcote, a small village two miles from Stratford. Mary brought with her an inheritance of sixty acres of land.

John Shakespeare was a glove-maker and dealer in wool, he may have at one time or another, pursued some other trades as well. He was a prosperous citizen of Stratford and one of its notables.

In the year of William Shakespeare's birth, however, his father was a prosperous businessman who was also a man of substance and of social standing. William, the third and surviving child of John and Mary Shakespeare was baptized on 26 April 1564. Allowing the usual period of three days between birth and baptism, it is generally assumed that William Shakespeare was born on 23 April 1564, which is also the day of the feast of St. George, the patron saint of England—and this is also the day on which Shakespeare breathed his last. The Shakespeares had five more children. It requires no documentary evidence to say that Shakespeare during his childhood observed and absorbed the life of town and village surging all around him and, possessing a rare talent, he stored in his mind sights, sounds, scenes and characters, which, combined with his experience of London, would prove a rich material at the forge of his creativity, when he came to write poems and plays.

There is no valid reason to doubt that William was enrolled in the local grammar school when he was six or seven years old. His father was still a prominent citizen and an important member of the borough council. But the school records for the period are not available. Nicholas Rowe, who brought out the first edited collection of Shakespeare's plays, wrote in his introduction that the boy studied in a free school where "it is probable, he acquired what Latin he was master of, but the narrowness of his circumstances, and the want of his assistance at home, forced his father to withdraw him from thence, and unhappily prevented his further proficiency in that language". John Aubrey a seventeenth-century antiquarian and biographer, in his *Brief Lives* published posthumously in 1813, informs us that Shakespeare had been a school master in a country school.

There is, however, no confusion regarding his early marriage to Anne Hathaway, who was about eight years his senior. One thing that can be safely inferred is that Shakespeare was an impetuous and highly romantic young man and this conclusion gets ample support in the essential nature of all his writings—they are romantic through and through. On 26th May 1583, their first issue Susanna was baptized in Stratford and two years later, the twins, Hamnet and Judith were born and christened on 2 February 1585. Of these children of Shakespeare, Hamnet died in 1596, Susanna married a physician named John Hall and inherited a major portion of her father's assets, Judith married Thomas Quiney.

The period from 1585 to 1592 in Shakespeare's life is known as the "dark years" or "lost years" from the biographer's point of view. For this period we have no authentic information about the family apart from a single reference to John Shakespeare in 1588 in connection with a legal dispute over a sum of money. There is, however, no dearth of legend and hearsay. According to Nicholas Rowe, Shakespeare incurred the wrath of the local landlord, Sir Thomas Lucy for stealing deer in his park and was, as a result, obliged to flee to London.

Though there are many conjectures, yet what sounds most credible is that Shakespeare attached himself to one of the touring theatrical companies that visited the countryside during the period under consideration. Three such companies, the Earl of Worcester's Men, the Earl of Oxford's Men and the Earl of Essex's Men, were giving performances at Stratford in 1581 and in 1585 the town people were entertained by an unidentified company. In 1587, the year in which Shakespeare most probably left his home town, the Earl of Essex's Men and the Earl of Leicester's Men were in Stratford; he might have accompanied one of these groups to London.

In the midst of financial and other problems besetting the family, joining a company of actors must have appealed to Shakespeare as a good expedient because it would bring some wages as well as give him an access to the literary world of London.

By 1592 Shakespeare's struggle had begun to bear fruit; in that year he was worthy enough to arouse the jealousy of another playwright, Robert Greene, one of the University Wits. In a letter addressed to his fellow writers and appended to a pamphlet called *Greene's Groatsworth of Wit Bought with a Million of Repentance* he made a scurrilous attack on Shakespeare for presuming to be not only an actor but the best playwright.

It is clear that by 1592 Shakespeare had established himself in London as an actor and dramatist: he had completed at least the three plays comprising the *Henry VI* trilogy; he had also probably been improving and retouching existing plays and there might have been some talk of his writing then in progress. Some scholars have argued that he had also completed or was about to complete *The Two Gentlemen of Verona, The Comedy of Errors, The Taming of the Shrew, Richard III, Titus Andronicus* and *Love's Labour's Lost.*

The next year, 1593, saw the publication of a long narrative poem, *Venus and Adonis*, with a signed dedication to Henry Wriothesley, the third Earl of Southampton: Your Honour's in all duty, William Shakespeare. In the following year came out another poem, *The Rape of Lucrece*, also dedicated to the same lord. This was the period during which the London theatres remained closed on account of the plague; that Shakespeare did not waste his time, but was busy writing poetry shows with what earnestness he pursued his aim of achieving literary renown. He had also started writing his sonnets during this period and some scholars have suggested that the group of sonnets addressed to a young man had the Earl of Southampton for their inspirator.

The theatres reopened in 1594 and staging of plays including some by Shakespeare began. We find that he is already an important member of Lord Chamberlain's company as disclosed by the following entry in the Chamber Accounts:

> To William Kemp, William Shakespeare, and Richard Burbage, servants to the Lord Chamberlain, upon the Council's warrant dated

> at Whitehall 15 March 1594 (-5) for two several comedies or interludes showed by them before her Majesty in Christmas time last past, *viz.* upon St. Stephen's day and Innocent's day, £ 13 6s, 8d, and by way of her Majesty's reward £ 6 13s, 4d.

From recorded references, allusions and lists of actors prefixed to printed plays, we gather that Shakespeare continued to act on the stage at least up to 1603 and if we rely on his fellow-actors, John Heminge and Henry Condell, who edited the First Folio edition of his plays in 1623, up to 1611. He is said to have played kingly roles including the Ghost in *Hamlet* but he also acted the part of old servant Adam in *As You Like It*. According to Aubrey, he "did act exceedingly well".

All the while Shakespeare was making steady progress in writing plays and in earning money and fame. During 1595-96, five of his new plays were produced: *Richard II, Romeo and Juliet, King John, A Midsummer Night's Dream,* and *The Merchant of Venice*. During the latter year there was a tragedy in the family: his only son Hamnet died in August 1596. In the same year, there was some more trouble for Shakespeare: according to a reference discovered by Leslie Hotson in 1931, one William Wayt claimed sureties of the peace against William Shakespeare and some other persons including Francis Langley then owner of the Swan Theatre. But his financial position was quite sound. He was living in a large house in Bishopsgate as the tax-rolls indicate, perhaps his family also stayed with him for brief periods. There is evidence of his purchase of property in London and in his hometown.

While living in London, Shakespeare appears to have maintained good links with his native place and its people. His narrative poems had been printed by Richard Field who had migrated from Stratford. In 1597 Shakespeare bought the largest house in Stratford, called New Place, from William Underhill for a sum of £ 60. On October 25, 1598, Richard Quiney a Stratford man who was visiting London wrote a letter to Shakespeare requesting a loan of £ 30. In 1599 the famous actor, Richard Burbage and his brother Cuthbert set up a new playhouse on the Bankside, called the Globe. Since they could not finance the project on their own, they invited some other members of their company, Lord Chamberlain's Men, to become shareholders. Shakespeare thus became a part-owner of the Globe, entitled to ten per cent of the profits. He enjoyed the unique privilege of being a dramatist, actor and businessman.

During the period 1597-99 six more plays comprising comedies and plays on English history were produced: *Merry Wives of Windsor, Much Ado About Nothing, As You Like It, Henry IV-Part One, Henry IV-Part Two,* and *Henry V*, probably *Julius Caesar* also had its first staging in 1599.

The new century opened with a personal tragedy to Shakespeare: his father died in 1601. It also brought him to the threshold of his tragic vision—the truest and profoundest ever presented to theatre audiences and to the readers of the world. Before the death of Queen Elizabeth in 1603, the greatest tragedy of personal dilemma *Hamlet* had its first performance. His finest comedy, *Twelfth Night* and the 'problem play' *Troilus and Cressida* were also produced before 1603. With the accession of King James to the English throne, Lord Chamberlain's Men, evidently regarded as the best company of actors, was taken under royal patronage and was renamed King's Men. The letters patent issued on 19 May 1603 mention William Shakespeare along with some other members of the company including Heminge and Condell, the future editors of the first edition of his Collected Plays. The actors of the company became eligible to special privileges; records indicate that they were often called upon to present plays before the Court and to participate in royal pageants and processions—several Shakespeare plays were performed at the Court. In March 1604, when King James made a 'royal proceeding' through the city of London, Shakespeare—as well as each of his fellow players—was given four yards of red cloth for his livery.

On the plane of worldly affairs too, Shakespeare was faring very well. In may 1602 he purchased one hundred and seven acres of arable land to the parish of old Stratford and in September he acquired a cottage in Chapel Lane, Stratford-on-

Avon. A fellow actor, Augustine Phillipps, when he made his will in May 1605, mentioned Shakespeare first among the recipients of his bequests of gold pieces: "I give and bequeath to my fellow, William Shakespeare, a thirty-shilling piece in gold." Two years later in 1607 his favourite daughter Susanna, married the physician John Hall and in February 1608 their daughter Elizabeth was born. It is almost certain that Edmond Shakespeare whose burial is recorded in the registers of the Church of St. Saviours in Southwark was the poet's brother. Shakespeare's mother died in 1608.

In Shakespeare's literary output, the period 1604-1608 is the period of great tragedies: *Othello, Macbeth, King Lear, Antony and Cleopatra* and *Cariolanus*. The other plays first produced during this period are: *Measure for Measure*, *All's Well That Ends Well* and *Timon of Athens*. Some scholars, however, believe that *All's Well That Ends Well* is an early play, perhaps *Love's Labour's Won*, mentioned by Francis Meres in his *Palladis Tamia* (1598).

In 1608 the King's Men took over the Blackfriars, an indoor theatre where Henry Evans's children's company had been staging plays since 1600. Shakespeare thus began writing plays for both Blackfriars and the Globe. He appears to have adjusted himself to the conditions and upper-class audiences at the Blackfriars. Otherwise, too, Shakespeare about this time had emerged from the Inferno of human and supernatural evil. He had explored the genesis, nature, working and consequences of evil and expressed them in the best of utterance. Now in the last phase of his career, he turned to superior kinds of solutions. Evil keeps raising its head, but it is confronted by higher human nature and is overthrown without waste or destruction. This is the tenor of his last plays: *Pericles, Cymbeline, The Winter's Tale, The Tempest.*

William Shakespeare had made his life a grand success: Whatever wrongs, malice, envy or injury he had suffered were behind him; he had become rich and respected; thousands of human hearts had been moved to laughter and tears by the magic of his lines; he had learnt the last lesson in human wisdom.

Around 1611 Shakespeare contentedly retired to Stratford. His remaining two younger brothers, Gilbert and Richard died in 1612 and 1613 respectively. John Combe, one of his closest friends also died in 1613 leaving him a bequest of £ 5. On March 10, 1613, he bought the Blackfriar's Gate House.

Shakespeare did not break his relations completely with his company; he also kept visiting London from time to time. The last two plays which he wrote in collaboration with John Fletcher are *Henry VII* and *The Two Noble Kinsmen*, but his heart wasn't there; they suffer in execution and in imaginative power. Shakespeare's health began to deteriorate after 1613. According to one report some time in 1616 Drayton and Ben Jonson came down to visit him and they had a merry meeting. His will was drawn up in January 1616. Since his younger daughter Judith got married to Thomas Quiney on February 10, the will was revised and executed by him on March 25.

In his will, Shakespeare bequeathed nearly all his property to his elder daughter Susanna Hall and her husband; Judith his younger daughter received very little in comparison. Perhaps Shakespeare was not happy with Judith's marriage to Thomas Quiney about whom there was some scandal, or, he feared any fixed assets made over to her would not remain secure, but he made provision for yearly payment of some money to her. This apparent lack of balance on the part of Shakespeare is bound to remind us of his own creation *King Lear*.

Another matter which causes surprise is the bequest to his wife. She is not mentioned by name and Shakespeare appears to have added one sentence about her as an after thought: "I give unto my wife my second best bed with the furniture". Those who defend Shakespeare on this issue argue that the best bed in the house would be reserved for guests, that he gave her the second best bed because it carried past associations since this must have been the bed the couple used to sleep in. It is also true that Anne's dower rights already stood protected bylaw; she must have continued to live in New Place until her death in 1623. And yet, when all this has been said, one cannot help feeling that this slighting gesture on the part of Shakespeare indicates that something had gone sour in their relations.

He left something to each of his relations: niece Elizabeth Hall, sister Joan and her three sons; he did not forget his friends and the poor of Stratford, to whom he bequeathed ten pounds. It is to be noted that he gave 26s. 8d. each to his former fellow actors, John Heminge, Richard Burbage and Henry Condell for buying mourning rings.

Shakespeare died on 23 April, 1616, but Death could not be proud of this, for in black ink his name still shines bright. A monument representing the poet in the act of writing with a quill was installed some time between his death and the year 1623. This is the famous bust with which the whole world has become familiar. The other authentic likeness is Martin Droeshout's engraving on the title page of the First Folio Collection of Shakespeare's Plays, which is equally familiar to readers. The epitaph inscribed under the bust praises Shakespeare as a writer.

With whome
Quick nature died; whose name doth deck
this tombe
Far more than most, sith all that He hath writt
Leaves living art, but page, to serve his witt.

KING LEAR
A CRITICAL INTRODUCTION

Among the tragedies of passion, *King Lear* is the one in which passions assume the largest proportions, act upon the widest theatre and attain their absolute extremes. The story of Lear and his daughters was found by Shakespeare in Holinshed and he may have taken a few hints from an old play, *The True Chronicle History of King Leir*. In both Holinshed's version and that of *The True Chronicle*, the army of Lear and his French allies is victorious; Lear in reinstated in his kingdom; but Holinshed relates how after Lear's death, her sister's sons warred against Cordelia and took her prisoner whereafter she slew herself. The story relating to Gloucester and his two sons Shakespeare took from Sir Philip Sidney's *Arcadia*. But Shakespeare turns the happily ending story in *Arcadia* to a tragedy. The date of the play is probably 1605 or 1606. It was entered on the Stationer's register on 26 November, 1607 and the entry states that it had been acted "upon St. Stephen's day at Christmas last," i.e., 26 December, 1606.

Good and evil in this play are clearly severed from one another, more so than in *Macbeth* or *Othello*, and in the ultimate analysis, goodness, if we merely judge by external fortune, would seem to be, if not defeated, at least not triumphant. Shakespeare has dared, while paying little regard to mere historical verisimilitude, to represent the most solemn and awful mysteries of life as they actually are, without attempting to offer a readymade explanation of them. Cordelia dies strangled in prison, yet we know that her devotion to love was not misspent. Lear expires in an agony of grief but he has been delivered from his pride and passionate willfulness: he has found that instead of being a master, at whose nod all things must bow, he is weak and helpless, a sport even of the wind and the rain; his ignorance of true love, and pleasure in false profession of love, have given place to an agonized clinging to love which is real, deep and tranquil because of its fullness. Lear is the greatest sufferer in Shakespeare's plays; though so old, he has strength which makes him a subject for prolonged and vast agony; and patience is unknown to him. The elements seem to have conspired against him with his unnatural daughters; the upheaval of the moral world, and the rage of tempest in the air seem to be parts of the same gigantic convulsion. In the midst of this tempest wanders unhoused the white-haired Lear; while his fool—most pathetic of all the minor characters of Shakespeare—jests half-widely, half coherently, half-bitterly, half-tenderly and always with a sad remembrance of the happier past. The poor boy's heard has been sore ever since his "young mistress went to France." If Cordelia is pure love, tender and faithful, and Kent is unmingled loyalty, the monsters Goneril and Regan are gorgons rather than women, such as Shakespeare has nowhere else conceived. The aspect of Goneril can almost turn to stone; in Regan's tongue there is a viperous hiss. The story of Gloucester enlarges the basis of the tragedy. Lear's affliction is no more private incident there is a breaking of the bonds of nature and society all around us. But Gloucester is suffering for a former sin of self-indulgence. Lear appears "more sinned against than sinning." Yet Gloucester is granted a death which is half joyful. His affliction serves as a measure of the longer affliction of the king. Edgar and Edmund are a contrasted pair—both are men of penetration, energy and skill, one on the side of evil, the other on the side of good. Everywhere throughout the play Shakespeare's imaginative daring impresses us. Nothing in poetry is bolder or more wonderful than the scene on the night of the tempest in the novel where the king, whose intellect has now given way, is in company with Edgar, assuming madness, the Fool, with his pathetic, forced mirth and Kent.

(i) THE PLAY IN RELATION TO OTHER TRAGEDIES

King Lear has quite often been regarded as the greatest work of Shakespeare. It lacks the popular fame of *Hamlet*, perhaps because it has a less enigmatic character. *Othello*, which perhaps appeared just before *Lear*, has more obvious cause for winning the readers'/audience's engagement. *Macbeth*, which is considered *Lear's* successor, has more splendid poetry. Nevertheless *Lear* incontrovertibly has much greater universality than either *Othello* or *Macbeth* or, for that matter, any other tragedy in English. The protagonist here is no assassin, nor is he the victim of an adversary's unimaginable malice but someone with inherent largeness of soul who suffers most disproportionately, partly by his own errors of judgement. The suffering is tragic rather than melodramatic and it raises the whole problem of evil. "Is there any cause in nature that makes these hard hearts?" (Act III; Scene vi; line 75). Is there justice in the world, or in the heavens? *Lear* goes farther than the other tragedies of Shakespeare in answering the problem by insisting on the value of endurance, and by showing us the hero purged through suffering. *Lear* is certainly a tragic reading of life but not a cynical one. The play leaves an impression that it is the quality of life rather than its quantity that matters. Nowhere in Shakespeare are 'integrity, loyalty, patience, love, forgiveness, humility' more powerfully presented than in *Lear*. Thus, the play, though not a religious work, is compatible with religion, which adds to its stature and appeal.

(ii) THE ATMOSPHERE IN *KING LEAR*

The clearest proof of the distinguishing feature of the atmosphere of the play is the manner in which a song of *Twelfth Night* has been employed in *King Lear*. The Fool, in the midst of the storm, sings a verse of the same song with which the clown closes that comedy and the verse sounds appropriate in the context of the pitiless night at the moor and the madness and sorrow of Lear.

> He that has, and a little tiny wit,—
> With hey, ho, the wind and the rain,—
> Must make content with his fortunes fit;
> Though the rain it raineth every day.

Twelfth Night was acted in 1601-02 and *King Lear* in 1605 or 1606. What did the playwright pass through during the intervening period? Passing through *Hamlet, Troilus 'and Cressida, Othello, Measure for Measure* and *Macbeth,* the terrible journey culminates in *Lear*. There is no drama in the whole range of modem literature which can equal the play in the tragic imagination which has clothed with chaotic darkness not merely Lear himself and other characters but also the whole of humanity, even the gods themselves. The loveliness of Cordelia's love and the loyal truth to Kent, and the tenderness of the Fool, and the pity of Lear's madness, while they redeem human nature from the horror of Regan and Edmund, Goneril and Cornwall, only deepen the dreadful aspect of the world, for they suffer for their goodness more than these vulture men and women for their crimes. It is also relevant to note that Shakespeare did emerge out of this dark tunnel. Like Dante, having seen hell and set Cordelia shining like a star above its brown and fiery airs, he climbed out of it and saw the stars again in *Cymbeline*, *Winter's Tale* and in *The Tempest*.

In *King Lear* the evils are those that characterise the beginnings of a society. Gloucester's light talk before his bastard son of his lust with his mother, the tearing out of Gloucester's eyes by Cornwall and Regan (the Woman urging on the horrible dead), the hanging of Cordelia, the lust for Edmund of both the sisters in an unabashed manner, the unnatural absence in Goneril and Regan of any shred of filial piety towards their father, rather the unrelenting cruelty to him—all show a society bereft of any trace of civilization or values, a primeval society incontrovertibly. Against the backdrop of such social scenery, the savagery of the powers that be is perhaps comprehensible. No Furies, not even the inward snake of Remorse haunt Goneril and Regan. They die of their own lust. And no God seems to inhabit *King Lear*; no divine Justice interposes to cuddle Cordelia. There are many who think Shakespeare ought to have saved her. But he was not in the temper to do that justice. The world is as it is, he perhaps reasoned, and the best for her, he thought, is that she should leave it. It is a stark world, unfit for those with weak stomachs and the only relief at the end of the day is the impression that the Furies unleashed have spent themselves and all would be quiet henceforth.

(iii) ACTWISE AND SCENEWISE PLOT OUTLINE OF THE PLAY

Act I; Scene (i): The ageing King of Britain, Lear, has decided to divide his kingdom in three parts. But he asks for an expression of love from his three daughters. The youngest, Cordelia, is his favourite but she fails to measure up to his high expectations. Her sincerity prevents her from using high-blown protestations of love. Lear, enraged, divides his kingdom between the other two daughters, Goneril and Regan, depriving Cordelia of her share. The Earl of Kent, the king's faithful follower protests at this injustice but is banished for his pains. The King of France accepts Cordelia as his wife without her dowry.

Act I; Scene (ii): Edmund, the illegitimate son of the Earl Gloucester, causes his father to suspect his true son, Edgar, of plotting against his life.

Act I; Scene (iii): Goneril complains to Oswald, her steward, about Lear's conduct and encourages him to allow the servants to be negligent in their service to him.

Act I; Scene (iv): Kent, in disguise, gets himself engaged in Lear's service and attacks Oswald. The Fool mingles with his jests shrewd comments on his master's folly. Goneril rebukes her father who in turn curses her and sends Oswald with a letter about him to her sister, Regan.

Act I; Scene (v): Lear prepares for going to Gloucester. Kent has gone ahead with Lear's letter to Regan.

Act II; Scene (i): Edmund falsely tells Gloucester that Edgar has wounded him for he refused to join Edgar's conspiracy against Gloucester. Regan, having received letters from both Goneril and her father, prefers to be at Gloucester's castle with her husband, Cornwall, when her father arrives.

Act II; Scene (ii): Kent's quarrel with Oswald continues for which Cornwall punishes Kent but Gloucester sympathizes with him.

Act II; Scene (iii): Edgar, in danger of his life, decides to disguise himself as a mad beggar.

Act II; Scene (iv): Lear is incensed at finding Kent in the stocks. Regan too is no less callous towards him. Goneril also arrives there and the two sisters refuse to receive Lear's followers into their houses. Lear, in disgust, walks out into the storm.

Act III; Scene (i): Kent, during his search for Lear, comes to know of the growing split between Albany and Cornwall and of the landing of an army from France.

Act III; Scene (ii): Kent finds Lear and the Fool out in the storm and he guides them to the shelter of a hovel.

Act III; Scene (iii): Gloucester reveals to Edmund where his sympathies lie.

Act III; Scene (iv): Lear, outside the hovel, feels pity for the common people, suffering the fury of Nature. He meets the disguised Edgar, feigning madness. Gloucester also joins them.

Act III; Scene (v): Edmund betrays his father to Cornwall, who promises Edmund earldom in return.

Act III; Scene (vi): Gloucester takes the victims of the storm into shelter. The mad king stages here a mock trial. Gloucester arranges to send Lear to Dover for safety.

Act III; Scene (vii): Gloucester is captured. Cornwall orders to have his eyes taken out as punishment for having served Lear. An outraged servant wounds him fatally.

Act IV; Scene (i): Edgar, in disguise, meets his now-humbled father, and offers to take him to Dover.

Act IV; Scene (ii): Goneril quarrels with her husband, Albany, over her fondness for Edmund.

Act IV; Scene (iii): Kent hears from an unnamed Gentleman how Cordelia received the news of her father's condition.

Act IV; Scene (iv): Cordelia sends out people in search of Lear.

Act IV; Scene (v): Regan seeks Oswald's help in marrying Edmund.

Act IV; Scene (vi): Edgar saves Gloucester from suicide. Lear exhibits 'reason in madness'. Edgar saves his father from Oswald who is killed but his dead body yields evidence of Goneril's conspiracy with Edmund.

Act IV; Scene (vii): Lear awakens to partial recovery of his wits, attended by Cordelia, Kent and a Doctor.

Act V; Scene (i): Regan and Goneril fight over Edmund. Edgar delivers a letter to Albany.

Act V; Scene (ii): Edgar goes to the battle and brings the news of the defeat of Lear and Cordelia.

Act V; Scene (iii): Lear and Cordelia discover each other, even as Edmund orders their execution. Edgar challenges Edmund and gives him a fatal wound. Goneril poisons Regan but as her intrigue with Edmund is exposed, she kills herself. Lear brings the strangled Cordelia and thinking that she lives, dies. Kent seems ready to follow his master. Albany and Edgar are left to manage the tangled state of affairs.

(iv) THE CHARACTERS IN THE PLAY

(a) Edmund

Characterized by a cool cruelty, it is Edmund who orders Cordelia to be hanged. Greedy of power and wealth, no motion of conscience troubles him till he has received his death wound. More than the primeval world which characterizes the play in general, Edmund seems a denizen of the Machiavellian self-interest which Shakespeare associates with Italy. Edmund's soliloquy about his bastardy, his claim to be the lusty child of Nature, his scorn of custom, convention and law, because he himself is an illegality; his call on the gods to stand up for bastards—all are instances of a certain recklessness rather than pre-civilization savagery. His deliberate and soulless treachery; his cunning and conscienceless conduct by which he sacrifices father and brother for his lust of power; his careful weighing whether Goneril's or Regan's love will be most to his advantage, without any love for either of them place him in a 'modern' world of conscious unscrupulousness. Edmund is aware of his own blackness. He sees and mocks at the self-excusing hypocrisy of society, not only in others but also in his own self. He consciously cultivates hypocrisy and treachery for self-advancement. Edmund hears the circumstances of his birth spoken of with a most degrading and licentious levity. The consciousness of the notoriety of his birth is the corrosive virus which innoculates pride with a venom, with hatred and a lust for power. The pangs of shame, personally undeserved, are perceived by him as wrongs. These turn him vindictive, especially against a brother whose stainless birth and honours were the constant remembrance of his own debasement.

(b) Edgar

Disguise proves to be a liberating factor for Edgar too. Though pink of propriety and thoroughly admirable in morals as well as manners, in disguise he lets loose the most original thoughts, the most unconventional things which his soul had mused on and concealed. All that we listen to from the lips of poor Tom lay buried under the outward reality of Edgar the man of society. The role of a madman he plays to perfection, so much did he seem to like it. The disguise is just not without any purpose in the play. Lear, who is half-mad, by then, discovers the strange reason at the back of Edgar's talk and he cries:

> "Noble philosopher, your company."
>
> ....
>
> "I will keep still with my philosopher."

Edgar himself is not the same man after he goes through the disguise. Having gone through misery, starvation and cold, he is more just in feeling, higher in intellectual insight, than he was in his luxurious days. At the close, his conduct is worthy of a noble gentleman who, while defending truth and loyalty, is tolerant to his false and treacherous brother when he is dying and a little repentant.

(c) Albany

It would be wrong to take him as of little importance in the play. Really he is the pivot on which the plane turns. He is central, in as much as he is the one character in the whole play who is from first to last completely sane, balanced, and normal. Sparing of words, unhurried and even slow in action, he is never either confused or hustled; and when the occasion arrives, he can strike with telling effect.

(d) Cordelia

Lear in an unjust manner draws attention to perhaps the central trait in Cordelia when he exclaims, "Let pride, which she calls plainness, marry her!" It would be inconceivable to have in a nature so strong as Cordelia's absence of a keen sense of dignity, pride and resentment. Cordelia's language to her sisters is little adapted to soften their hearts towards their father. Similar is the case as she and her father are brought in, prisoners, to the enemy's camp. She obviously could not have brought herself to plead with her sisters for her father's life.

(e) Kent

Unlike the smooth and suave Edmund, Kent is the plain, faithful man who has never minced his words nor filed his mind. When in disguise, he exaggerates all the more his plainness of speech, as if he feels let loose from the restraints of his high position. His attack on Oswald, whom he abhors for his flattery and knavery, is ferocious, but it delights him to make it. No servant but one in disguise could have made it. Despite all his bluntness, he is as tender as he is faithful. He never leaves the king who has banished him; tends him like a nurse through storm and madness, and Cordelia is always in his heart. It is his love of Lear, Gloucester and Cordelia which finally leads to the cracking of his strings of life. Kent says but little as the Earl of Kent in the play, but it is he who conducts most of the affairs in the play. He is one of those steadfast men, with the gift of fidelity to persons and to long established ideals, and with the gift of silent common sense, who, when the affairs are stormy, holds the fort quietly, directs the ship and brings it safely to land. One should not be misled by the opulence of abusive words and the torrent of talk which issues forth from him when he is in disguise. It is pertinent to recall here Kent's trouncing of Oswald in the courtyard scene. Such conduct is but the liberating impact of the disguise one puts on.

(f) The Fool

The function of the Fool in the play is closely related to the spiritual process and meaning of the play. It is the Fool's business to goad Lear, to stir his conscience, to make him realize the situation he is in. Lear walks in a world of illusions; the Fool walks beside him like a reflection of the truth. His speech, full of homely, vivid figures, heightens the attractiveness of his part, makes it more credible, yet softens the irritation of his persistent goading. He could not reach the king with argument but he can by a homely image. Significantly enough, all the Fool's talk is with Lear and he is literally Lear's fool. Truth and wisdom and love, the Fool knows and Lear is to discover, are by-products of living not objectives to be reached by calculation. The Fool's appearance on the scene with wisdom of the kind not provided for in our categories is greatly satisfying to us. The Fool is a comforting reminder of the fact that there is more wisdom to be acquired by the process of living than we have been able to acquire with all our directed cerebration.

(g) Lear

Lear's figure haunts us like few other figures do. What is his tragic flaw or why does he suffer the fate he is shown suffering in the play. His only failing seems to be his over-confidence in his judgement. He has, without one check, ruled for many years his kingdom and his household and he thinks that his will is absolute wisdom. To put it differently, in playing his role as a king for such a long period, he forgets/subordinates his role as a parent, dealing with his children as if they were his subjects. He is blind to his own folly; blind to the fact that his two daughters hate him; blind when their embroidered protestations he takes as sincere expressions of love; blind to the worth of the unassuming Cordelia; blind to the loyalty of Kent; blind to the political fallout of his impulsive partition of the kingdom, even if his daughters had really loved him; blind to the consequences of his moving from one petty court to another in a dependent position with a train of a hundred knights. Lear's tragedy emanates from this single foible, howsoever innocuous it may seem in itself.

To believe that Lear was already mad when he acted unreasonably would imply equating vanity to insanity. Lear is a healthy giant of a man, given to hunting and feasting and drinking. There is no physical or mental feebleness suggested as we meet him in the first scene. It is no half-paralysed old man, but a giant smitten to the heart who is finally broken down by those whose love he had cherished and therefore, hostility from these quarters was the bitterest blow to him. It is only after fearful and redoubled shocks which subvert everything he has believed, and after a protracted struggle against their maddening assault that he finally loses his will power over his brain. And even then, it is complete madness only for a time. He slips in and out of madness. Even though he is himself exhausted and close to his breaking point, Lear realizes that Edgar's raving show of madness has strange reason at its back. He cries:

> "Noble philosopher, your company.
>
> ....
>
> "I will keep still with my philosopher."

Edgar, himself, listening to his wild talk near Dover, exclaims:

> "O, matter and impertinency mix'd!
> Reason in madness!"

Lear changes in the play from bursts of passion to quiet entreaty. Beaten to and fro from the weather of fury to the weather of self-control, and in the contest, fearing to be mad till at last he knows that all is useless and that his mind is breaking. "O fool! I shall go mad!" he cries and rushes out into the tempest. When we meet him again, on the moor and in the storm, he is not yet mad, nor weak of body. The tempest in his heart has heightened, for the moment all his powers. He sees not only himself but the fate and sorrow and crime of the whole world. No madness as yet—but the intellect at its highest range and the emotions at their tensest strain. And the last straw is the entrance of Edgar who plays the madman. Lear lets loose his self-command and becomes a spirit brother of Edgar.

The scene on the black and lonely moor is pictorial as few scenes are in literature. We are presented the landscape, the night, the lightnings and the rain, Lear among them with his white hair upon the wind, the fool, Kent, the hovel, Edgar—not by stock phrases and routine expressions, but by the flying words which glance across the passions and thoughts of the men. Lear's passion is louder and fiercer than the material storm. The fool's wild jesting gives a fresh wildness to the raging elements and to Lear. Edgar's imitative madness fires Lear's incipient loss of control. Last but not least Gloucester slips into add his own half-insane sorrow to the dreadful night.

Out of this all-pervasive chaos, Lear emerges in a refreshingly new light. He thinks perhaps for the very first time in his life of the dreadful state of the world rather than of his own self. He pierces deep into the hidden blackness of mankind. His speeches are dark with the unlighted, hopeless vision of life that sets this play apart. When he thinks of his own anger and pain, he is brought, as never before, to think of the pains of others. Out of a ruined king's mouth is thus heard the starkest judgement on the pettiness of the great and the unbearable misery of the poor:

> "Poor naked wretches, whereso'er you are,
> That bide the pelting of this pitiless storm,
> How shall your houseless heads, and unfed sides,
> Your loop'd and window'd raggedness, defend you
> From seasons such as these? O, I have taken
> Too little care of this?"

From this juncture Lear has but to take a couple of steps only to the ending. Edgar's entrance in imitated madness wakes the latent madness in Lear. Lear takes to him at once. He pities him. He calls Edgar his learned Theban, his Athenian, his philosopher. It is only when Cordelia comes to Lear and comforts him that Lear is brought back to his self. As Cordelia watches him, he sleeps. The scene is heart-rendering. Lear kneels before her. When she protests, "No, Sir, you must not kneel", he exclaims:

"Pray do not mock me:
I am a very foolish fond old man,
....
I fear I am not in my perfect mind."

He continues in the same vein:

"If you have poison for me, I will drink it.
I know you do not love me; for your sisters
Have, as I do remember, done me wrong:
You have some cause, they have not."

As Cordelia mutters, "No cause, no cause," Shakespeare reaches the divine simplicity of passion that can ever be conveyed in words. However, it would be too much to expect that a happy ending could terminate such unfolding of action. Goneril, Regan, Cornwall, Edmund—all have died violently. Cordelia and Lear must meet as violent a death. Cordelia is hanged, ignobly hanged by one as merciless as Regan. Cordelia hits the key-note as she is taken away:

"We are not the first
Who with best meaning have incurred the worst"

Lear, too, is happy in that he has finally discovered, he believes, love:

"Come, let's away to prison;
We two alone will sing like birds i'the cage."

But it is his last hour of happiness. We next see him seized by frenzy, with Cordelia dead in his arms. At last his heart breaks asunder; imagining that her lips are still fumbling for words, he finally dies. The mighty titan with a child's heart, though not spotlessly guiltless, dies child-like. The final words about him neatly convey the general impression about him:

"Vex not his ghost: O, let him pass! he hate him
That would upon the rack of this tough world
Stretch him out longer."

THE TRAGEDY OF KING LEAR

THE ACTORS' NAMES

Lear, King of Britain
King of France
Duke of Burgundy
Duke of Cornwall
Duke of Albany
Earl of Kent
Earl of Gloucester
Edgar, Son to Gloucester
Edmund, Bastard Son to Gloucester
Curan, a Courtier
Old Man, Tenant to Gloucester
Doctor
Fool
Oswald, Steward to Goneril
A Capital employed by Edmund
Gentleman, attendant on Cordelia
A Herald
Servants to Cornwall

Goneril, Regan, Cordelia,	daughter to Lear

I.1

Enter Kent, Gloucester and Bastard.

KENT: I thought the King had more affected the Duke of Albany, than Cornwall.

GLOUCESTER: It did always seem so to us: but now in the division of the Kingdom, it appears not which of the dukes he values most, for equalities are so weigh'd, that curiosity in neither, can make choice of either's moiety.

KENT: Is not this your son, my Lord?

GLOUCESTER: His breeding, sir, hath been at my charge. I have so often blush'd to acknowledge him, that now I am braz'd to't.

KENT: I cannot conceive you.

GLOUCESTER: Sir, this young fellow's mother could; whereupon she grew round-womb'd, and had indeed, sir, a son for her cradle, ere she had a husband for her bed. Do you smell a fault?

KENT: I cannot wish the fault undone, the issue of it, being so proper.

GLOUCESTER: But I have a son, sir, by order of Law, some year elder than this; who, yet is no dearer in my account, though this knave came something saucily into the world before he was sent for: yet was his mother fair, there was good sport at his making, and the whoreson must be acknowledged. Do you know this noble gentleman, Edmund?

BASTARD: No, my Lord.

GLOUCESTER: My Lord of Kent: remember him hereafter, as my honourable friend.

BASTARD: My services to your Lordship.

KENT: I must love you, and sue to know you better.

BASTARD: Sir, I shall study deserving.

GLOUCESTER: He hath been out nine years, and away he shall again. The King is coming.

Sound a Sennet. Enter one bearing a Coronet; then Lear; then the Dukes of Albany and Cornwall; next Goneril, Regan, and Cordelia; with followers.

LEAR: Attend the Lords of France and Burgundy, Gloucester.

GLOUCESTER: I shall, my Lord.

Exeunt Gloucester and Edmund.

LEAR: Meantime we shall express our darker purpose.
Give me the map there. Know, that we have divided
In three our Kingdom: and 'tis our fast intent,
To shake all cares and business from our age,
Conferring them on younger strengths, while we
Unburthen'd crawl toward death. Our son of Cornwall,
And you our no less loving son of Albany,
We have this hour a constant will to publish
Our daughters' several dowers, that future strife
May be prevented now. The Princes, France and Burgundy,
Great rivals in our youngest daughter's love,
Long in our Court, have made their amorous sojourn,
And here are to be answer'd. Tell me my daughters
(Since now we will divest us both of rule,
Interest of territory, cares of state)
Which of you shall we say doth love us most,
That we, our largest bounty may extend
Where Nature doth with merit challenge. Goneril,
Our eldest born, speak first.

GONERIL: Sir, I love you more than word can wield the matter,
Dearer than eye-sight, space, and liberty,
Beyond what can be valued, rich or rare,
No less than life, with grace, health, beauty, honour:
As much as child e'er lov'd, or father found.
A love that makes breath poor, and speech unable,
Beyond all manner of so much I love you.

CORDELIA: What shall Cordelia speak? Love, and be silent.

LEAR: Of all these bounds even from this line, to this,
With shadowy forests, and with champains rich'd,
With plenteous rivers, and wide-skirted meads,

We make thee Lady. To thine and Albany's issues
Be this perpetual. What says our second daughter?
Our dearest Regan, wife to Cornwall?
REGAN: I am made of that self metal as my sister
And prize me at her worth. In my true heart,
I find she names my very deed of love:
Only she comes too short, that I profess
Myself an enemy to all other joys,
Which the most precious square of sense possesses,
And find I am alone felicitate
In your dear Highness' love.
CORDELIA: Then poor Cordelia,
And yet not so, since I am sure my love's
More ponderous than my tongue.
LEAR: To thee, and thine hereditary ever,
Remain this ample third of our fair Kingdom,
No less in space, validity, and pleasure
Than that conferr'd on Goneril. Now our Joy,
Although our last and least; to whose young love,
The vines of France, and milk of Burgundy,
Strive to be interess'd. What can you say, to draw
A third, more opulent than your sisters? Speak.
CORDELIA: Nothing my Lord.
LEAR: Nothing?
CORDELIA: Nothing.
LEAR: Nothing will come of nothing, speak again.
CORDELIA: Unhappy that I am, I cannot heave
My heart into my mouth: I love your Majesty
According to my bond, no more nor less.
LEAR: How, how Cordelia? Mend your speech a little,
Lest it may mar your Fortunes.
CORDELIA: Good my Lord,
You have begot me, bred me, lov'd me.
I return those duties back as are right fit,
Obey you, love you, and most honour you.
Why have my sisters husbands, if they say

They love you all? Happily when I shall wed,
That Lord, whose hand must take my plight, shall carry
Half my love with him, half my care, and duty,
Sure I shall never marry like my sisters
[To love my father all.]
LEAR: But goes thy heart with this?
CORDELIA: Ay my good Lord.
LEAR: So young, and so untender?
CORDELIA: So young my Lord, and true.
LEAR: Let it be so, thy truth then be thy dower:
For by the sacred radiance of the sun,
The mysteries of Hecate and the night:
By all the operation of the orbs,
From whom we do exist, and cease to be,
Here I disclaim all my paternal care,
Propinquity and property of blood,
And as a stranger to my heart and me,
Hold thee from this for ever. The barbarous Scythian,
Or he that makes his generation messes
To gorge his appetite, shall to my bosom
Be as well neighbour'd, pitied, and reliev'd,
As thou my sometime daughter.
KENT: Good my Liege.
LEAR: Peace Kent,
Come not between the Dragon and his wrath,
I lov'd her most, and thought to set my rest
On her kind nursery. Hence and avoid my sight:
So be my grave my peace, as here I give
Her father's heart from her; call France; who stirs?
Call Burgundy. Cornwall, and Albany,
With my two daughters' dowers, digest this third;
Let pride, which she calls plainness, marry her:
I do invest you jointly with my power,
Pre-eminence, and all the large effects
That troop with majesty. Ourself by monthly course,
With reservation of an hundred knights,

By you to be sustain'd, shall our abode
Make with you by due turns, only we shall retain
The name, and all th' additions to a King:
The sway, revenue, execution of the rest,
Beloved sons be yours, which to confirm,
This coronet part beween you.
KENT: Royal Lear,
Whom I have ever honour'd as my King,
Lov'd as my father, as my master follow'd,
As my great patron thought on in my prayers.
LEAR: The bow is bent and drawn, make from the shaft.
KENT: Let it fall rather, though the fork invade
The region of my heart, be Kent unmannerly,
When Lear is mad, what wouldst thou do old man?
Think'st thou that duty shall have dread to speak,
When power to flattery bows? To plainness honour's bound,
When majesty falls to folly; reserve thy state,
And in thy best consideration, check
This hideous rashness, answer my life, my judgement:
Thy youngest daughter does not love thee least,
Nor are those empty-hearted, whose low sounds
Reverb no hollowness.
LEAR: Kent, on thy life no more.
KENT: My life I never held but as a pawn
To wage against thine enemies, ne'er fear to lose it,
Thy safety being the motive.
LEAR: Out of my sight.
KENT: See better Lear, and let me still remain
The true blank of thine eye.
LEAR: Now by Apollo.
KENT: Now by Apollo, King,
Thou swear'st thy Gods in vain.
LEAR: O, vassal! Miscreant.
ALBANY, CORNWALL: Dear sir forbear.
KENT: Kill thy physician, and thy fee bestow

Upon the foul disease, revoke thy gift,
Or whilst I can vent clamour from my throat,
I'll tell thee thou dost evil.

LEAR: Hear me recreant, on thine allegiance hear me;
Since thou hast sought to make us break our vows,
Which we durst never yet; and with strain'd pride,
To come between our sentences, and our power,
Which, nor our nature, nor our place can bear;
Our potency made good, take thy reward.
Five days we do allot thee for provision,
To shield thee from disasters of the world,
And on the sixth to turn thy hated back
Upon our kingdom; if on the tenth day following,
Thy banish'd trunk be found in our Dominions,
The moment is thy death, away. By Jupiter,
This shall not be revok'd.

KENT: Fare thee well, King, sith thus thou wilt appear,
Freedom lives hence, and banishment is here;
The Gods to their dear shelter take thee maid,
That justly think'st, and hast most rightly said:
And your large speeches, may your deeds approve,
That good effects may spring from words of love:
Thus Kent, O Princes, bids you all adieu,
He'll shape his old course, in a country new.

Exit.

Flourish. Enter Gloucester with France and Burgundy, Attendants.

GLOUCESTER: Here's France and Burgundy, my noble Lord.

LEAR: My Lord of Burgundy,
We first address toward you, who with this King
Hath rivall'd for our daughter: what in the least
Will you require in present dower with her,
Or cease your quest of love?

BURGUNDY: Most Royal Majesty,
I crave no more than hath your Highness offer'd,
Nor will you tender less?

LEAR: Right noble Burgundy,
When she was dear to us, we did hold her so,
But now her price is fallen: sir, there she stands,
If aught within that little seeming substance,
Or all of it with our displeasure piec'd,
And nothing more may fitly like your Grace,
She's there, and she is yours.
BURGUNDY: I know no answer.
LEAR: Will you with those infirmities she owes,
Unfriended, new-adopted to our hate,
Dower'd with our curse, and stranger'd with our oath,
Take her, or leave her?
BURGUNDY: Pardon me royal sir,
Election makes not up in such conditions.
LEAR: Then leave her sir, for by the power that made me,
I tell you all her wealth. For you great King,
I would not from your love make such a stray,
To match you where I hate, therefore beseech you
T' avert your liking a more worthier way,
Than on a wretch whom Nature is asham'd
Almost t' acknowledge hers.
FRANCE: This is most strange,
That she whom even but now, was your best object,
The argument of your praise, balm of your age,
Most best, the dearest, should in this trice of time
Commit a thing so monstrous, to dismantle
So many folds of favour: sure her offence
Must be of such unnatural degree,
That monsters it: or your fore-vouch'd affection
Fall into taint, which to believe of her
Must be a faith that reason without miracle
Should never plant in me.
CORDELIA: I yet beseech your Majesty.
If for I want that glib and oily art,
To speak and purpose not, since what I well intend,
I'll do 't before I speak, that you make known

It is no vicious blot, murther, or foulness,
No unchaste action, or dishonour'd step
That hath depriv'd me of your grace and favour,
But even for want of that, for which I am richer,
A still-soliciting eye, and such a tongue,
That I am glad I have not, though not to have it,
Hath lost me in your liking.

LEAR: Better thou
Hadst not been born, than not t' have pleas'd me better.

FRANCE: Is it but this? A tardiness in nature,
Which often leaves the history unspoke
That it intends to do: My Lord of Burgundy,
What say you to the lady? Love's not love
When it is mingled with regards, that stands
Aloof from th' intire point, will you have her?
She is herself a dowry.

BURGUNDY: Royal King,
Give but that portion which yourself propos'd,
And here I take Cordelia by the hand,
Duchess of Burgundy.

LEAR: Nothing, I have sworn, I am firm.

BURGUNDY: I am sorry then you have so lost a father.
That you must lose a husband.

CORDELIA: Peace be with Burgundy,
Since that respect and Fortune are his love,
I shall not be his wife.

FRANCE: Fairest Cordelia, that art most rich being poor,
Most choice forsaken, and most love'd, despis'd,
Thee and thy virtues here I seize upon,
Be it lawful I take up what's cast away.
Gods, Gods! 'Tis strange, that from their cold'st neglect
My love should kindle to inflam'd respect.
Thy dowerless daughter King, thrown to my chance,
Is Queen of us, of ours, and our fair France:
Not all the Dukes of wat'rish Burgundy,
Can buy this unpriz'd precious maid of me.

Bid them farewell Cordelia, though unkind,
Thou losest here a better where to find.
LEAR: Thou hast her France, let her be thine, for we
Have no such daughter, nor shall ever see
That face of hers again, therefore be gone,
Without our grace, our love, our benison:
Come noble Burgundy.
Flourish. Exeunt all but France, Goneril, Regan, and Cordelia.
FRANCE: Bid farewell to your sisters.
CORDELIA: The jewels of our father, with wash'd eyes
Cordelia leaves you, I know you what you are,
And like a sister am most loath to call
Your faults as they are named. Love well our father:
To your professed bosoms I commit him,
But yet alas, stood I within his grace,
I would prefer him to a better place,
So farewell to you both.
REGAN: Prescribe not us our duties.
GONERIL: Let your study
Be to content your Lord, who hath receiv'd you
At Fortune's alms; you have obedience scanted,
And well are worth the want that you have wanted.
CORDELIA: Time shall unfold what plighted cunning hides,
Who cover faults, at last with shame derides:
Well may you prosper.
FRANCE: Come my fair Cordelia.
Exeunt France and Cordelia.

GONERIL: Sister, it is not a little I have to say, of what most nearly appertains to us both; I think our father will hence to-night.

REGAN: That's most certain, and with you: next month with us.

GONERIL: You see how full of changes his age is, the observation we have made of it hath not been little; he always love'd our sister most, and with what poor judgement he hath now cast her off, appears too grossly.

REGAN: 'Tis the infirmity of his age, yet he hath ever but slenderly known himself.

GONERIL: The best and soundest of his time hath been but rash, then must we look to receive from his age, to receive not alone the imperfections of long-engraffed condition, but therewithal the unruly waywardness, that infirm and choleric years bring with them.

REGAN: Such unconstant starts are we like to have from him, as this of Kent's banishment.

GONERIL: There is further compliment of leave-taking between France and him, pray you let's sit together, if our father carry authority with such dispositions as he bears, this last surrender of his will but offend us.

REGAN: We shall further think of it.

GONERIL: We must do something, and i' th' heat.

Exeunt.

I.2

Enter Bastard.

BASTARD: Thou Nature art my Goddess; to thy Law
My services are bound, wherefore should I
Stand in the plague of custom, and permit
The curiosity of Nations, to deprive me?
For that I am some twelve, or fourteen moonshines
Lag of a brother? Why bastard? Wherefore base?
When my dimensions are as well compact,
My mind as generous, and my shape as true
As honest madam's issue? Why brand they us
With base? With baseness bastardy? Base, base?
Who in the lusty stealth of Nature, take
More composition, and fierce quality,
Than doth within a dull stale tired bed

Go to th' creating a whole tribe of fops
Got 'tween a sleep and wake? Well then,
Legitimate Edgar, I must have your land;
Our father's love, is to the bastard Edmund,
As to th' legitimate: fine word: legitimate.
Well, my legitimate, if this letter speed,
And my invention thrive, Edmund the base
Shall to th' legitimate: I grow, I prosper:
Now Gods, stand up for bastards.

Enter Gloucester.

GLOUCESTER: Kent banish'd thus and France in choler parted?
And the King gone to-night? Prescrib'd his power,
Confin'd to exhibition? All this done
Upon the gad? Edmund, how now? What news?

BASTARD: So please your Lordship, none.

GLOUCESTER: Why so earnestly seek you to put up that letter?

BASTARD: I know no news, my Lord.

GLOUCESTER: What paper were you reading?

BASTARD: Nothing my Lord.

GLOUCESTER: No? What needed then that terrible dispatch of it into your pocket? The quality of nothing, hath not such need to hide itself. Let's see: come, if it be nothing, I shall not need spectacles.

BASTARD: I beseech you sir, pardon me; it is a letter from my brother, that I have not all o'er-read; and for so much as I have perus'd, I find it not fit for your o'er-looking.

GLOUCESTER: Give me the letter, sir.

BASTARD: I shall offend, either to detain, or give it: the contents, as in part I understand them, are to blame.

GLOUCESTER: Let's see, let's see.

BASTARD: I hope for my brother's justification, he wrote this but as an essay, or taste of my virtue.

GLOUCESTER reads: *This policy, and reverence of age, makes the world bitter to the best of our times: keeps our fortunes from us, till our oldness cannot relish them. I begin to find an idle and fond bondage, in the oppression of aged tyranny, who sways not as it hath power, but as it is suffer'd. Come to me, that of this I may speak more. If our father would sleep till I wak'd him, you should enjoy half his revenue for ever, and live the beloved of your brother.* EDGAR

Hum? Conspiracy? Sleep till I wake him, you should enjoy half his revenue: my son Edgar, had he a hand to write this? A heart and brain to breed it in? When came you to this? Who brought it?

BASTARD: It was not brought me, my Lord; there's the cunning of it. I found it thrown in at the casement of my closet.

GLOUCESTER: You know the character to be your brother's?

BASTARD: If the matter were good my Lord, I durst swear it were his: but in respect of that, I would fain think it were not.

GLOUCESTER: It is his.

BASTARD: It is his hand, my Lord: but I hope his heart is not in the contents.

GLOUCESTER: Has he never before sounded you in this business?

BASTARD: Never, my Lord. But I have heard him oft maintain it to be fit, that sons at perfect age, and fathers declin'd, the father should be as ward to the son, and the son manage his revenue.

GLOUCESTER: O villain, villain: his very opinion in the letter. Abhorred villain, unnatural, detested, brutish villain; worse than brutish: go sirrah, seek him: I'll apprehend him. Abominable villain, Where is he?

BASTARD: I do not well know my Lord. If it shall please you to suspend your indignation against my brother, till you can derive from him better testimony of his intent, you should run a certain course: where, if you violently proceed against him, mistaking his purpose, it would make a great gap in your own honour, and shake in pieces, the heart of his obedience. I dare pawn down my life for him, that he hath writ this to feel my affection to your honour, and to no other pretence of danger.

GLOUCESTER: Think you so?

BASTARD: If your honour judge it meet, I will place you where you shall hear us confer of this, and by an auricular assurance have your satisfaction, and that without any further delay, than this very evening.

GLOUCESTER: He cannot be such a monster.

[BASTARD: Nor is not sure.

GLOUCESTER: To his father, that so tenderly and entirely loves him, Heaven and Earth!] Edmund seek him out: wind me into him, I pray you: frame the business after your own wisdom. I would unstate myself, to be in a due resolution.

BASTARD: I will seek him sir, presently: convey the business as I shall find means, and acquaint you withal.

GLOUCESTER: These late eclipses in the sun and moon portend no good to us: though the wisdom of Nature can reason it thus, and thus, yet Nature finds itself scourg'd by the sequent effects. Love cools, friendship falls off, brothers divide. In cities, mutinies; in countries, discord; in palaces, treason; and the bond crack'd, 'twixt son and father. This villain of mine comes under the prediction; there's son against father; the King falls from bias of Nature, there's father against child. We have seen the best of our time. Machinations, hollowness, treachery, and all ruinous disorders follow us disquietly to our graves. Find out this villain, Edmund, it shall lose thee nothing, do it carefully: and the noble and true-hearted Kent banish'd; his offence, honesty. 'Tis strange.

Exit.

BASTARD: This is the excellent foppery of the world, that when we are sick in fortune, often the surfeits of our own behaviour, we make guilty of our disasters, the sun, the moon, and stars, as if we were villains on necessity, fools by heavenly compulsion, knaves, thieves, and treachers by spherical predominance. Drunkards, liars, and adulterers, by an inforc'd obedience of planetary influence; and all that we are evil in, by a divine thrusting on. An admirable evasion of whoremaster man, to lay his goatish disposition on the charge of a star. My father compounded with my mother under the Dragon's tail, and my nativity was under *Ursa Major*, so that it follows, I am rough and lecherous. I should have been that I am, had the maidenliest star in the firmament twinkled on my bastardizing.

Enter Edgar.

Pat: he comes like the catastrophe of the old comedy: my cue is villanous melancholy, with a sigh like Tom o' Bedlam. —O these eclipses do portend these divisions. Fa, sol, la, mi.

EDGAR: How now brother Edmund, what serious contemplation are you in?

BASTARD: I am thinking brother of a prediction I read this other day, what should follow these eclipses.

EDGAR: Do you busy yourself about that?

BASTARD: I promise you, the effects he writes of, succeed unhappily, [as of unnaturalness between the child and the parent, death, dearth, dissolutions of ancient amities; divisions in state, menaces and maledictions against King and nobles, needless diffidences, banishment of friends, dissipation of cohorts, nuptial breaches, and I know not what.

EDGAR: How long have you been a sectary astronomical?

BASTARD: Come, come,] when saw you my father last?

EDGAR: The night gone by.

BASTARD: Spake you with him?

EDGAR: Ay, two hours together.

BASTARD: Parted you in good terms? Found you no displeasure in him, by word, or countenance?

EDGAR: None at all.

BASTARD: Bethink yourself wherein you may have offended him: and at my entreaty forbear his presence, until some little time hath qualified the heat of his displeasure, which at this instant so rageth in him, that with the mischief of your person, it would scarcely allay.

EDGAR: Some villain hath done me wrong.

BASTARD: That's my fear, I pray you have a continent forbearance till the speed of his rage goes slower: and as I say, retire with me to my lodging, from whence I will fitly bring you to hear my Lord speak: pray ye go, there's my key: if you do stir abroad, go arm'd.

EDGAR: Arm'd, brother?

BASTARD: Brother, I advise you to the best, I am no honest man, if there be any good meaning toward you: I have told you what I have seen, and heard: but faintly. Nothing like the image, and horror of it, pray you away.

EDGAR: Shall I hear from you anon?

Exit.

BASTARD: I do serve you in this business:
A credulous father, and a brother noble,
Whose nature is so far from doing harms,
That he suspects none: on whose foolish honesty
My practices ride easy: I see the business.
Let me, if not by birth, have lands by wit,
All with me's meet, that I can fashion fit.

Exit.

I.3

Enter Goneril, and Steward.

GONERIL: Did my father strike my gentleman for chiding of his fool?

STEWARD: Ay Madam.

GONERIL: By day and night, he wrongs me, every hour
He flashes into one gross crime, or other,
That sets us all at odds: I'll not endure it;
His knights grow riotous, and himself upbraids us
On every trifle. When he returns from hunting,
I will not speak with him, say I am sick.
If you come slack of former services,
You shall do well, the fault of it I'll answer.

STEWARD: He's coming, Madam, I hear him.

GONERIL: Put on what weary negligence you please,
You and your fellows: I'll have it come to question;
If he distaste it, let him to our sister,

Whose mind and mine, I know in that are one,
[Not to be over-ruled; idle old man
That still would manage those authorities
That he hath given away, now by my life,
Old fools are babes again, and must be us'd
With cheques as flatteries, when they are seen abus'd.]
Remember what I tell you.

STEWARD: Well Madam.

GONERIL: And let his knights have colder looks among you:
What grows of it no matter, advise your fellows so,
[I would breed from hence occasions, and I shall,
That I may speak], I'll write straight to my sister
To hold my very course; prepare for dinner.

Exeunt.

I.4

Enter Kent.

KENT: If but as well I other accents borrow,
That can my speech defuse, my good intent
May carry through itself to that full issue
For which I raz'd my likeness. Now banish'd Kent,
If thou canst serve where thou dost stand condemn'd,
So may it come, thy master whom thou lov'st,
Shall find thee full of labours.

Horns within. Enter Lear and Attendants.

LEAR: Let me not stay a jot for dinner, go get it ready: how now, what art thou?

KENT: A man, sir.

LEAR: What dost thou profess? What wouldst thou with us?

KENT: I do profess to be no less than I seem; to serve him truly that will put me in trust, to love him that is honest, to converse with him that is wise and says little, to fear judgement, to fight when I cannot choose, and to eat no fish.

LEAR: What art thou?

KENT: A very honest-hearted fellow, and as poor as the King.

LEAR: If thou be'st as poor for a subject as he's for a King, thou art poor enough. What wouldst thou?

KENT: Service.

LEAR: Who wouldst thou serve?

KENT: You.

LEAR: Dost thou know me fellow?

KENT: No sir, but you have that in your countenance, which I would fain call master.

LEAR: What's that?

KENT: Authority.

LEAR: What services canst thou do?

KENT: I can keep honest counsel, ride, run, mar a curious tale in telling it, and deliver a plain message bluntly: that which ordinary men are fit for, I am qualified in, and the best of me, is diligence.

LEAR: How old art thou?

KENT: Not so young sir to love a woman for singing, nor so old to dote on her for any thing: I have years on my back forty eight.

LEAR: Follow me, thou shalt serve me, if I like thee no worse after dinner, I will not part from thee yet. Dinner ho, dinner; where's my knave? my fool? Go you and call my fool hither.

Enter Steward.

You you sirrah, where's my daughter?

STEWARD: So please you—

Exit.

LEAR: What says the fellow there? Call the clotpoll back: where's my fool? Ho, I think the world's asleep, how now? Where's that mongrel?

KNIGHT: He says my Lord, your daughter is not well.

LEAR: Why came not the slave back to me when I call'd him.

KNIGHT: Sir, he answered me in the roundest manner, he would not.

LEAR: He would not?

KNIGHT: My Lord, I know not what the matter is, but to my judgement your Highness is not entertain'd with that ceremonious affection as you were wont, there's a great abatement of kindness appears as well in the general dependants, as in the duke himself also, and your daughter.

LEAR: Ha? Sayest thou so?

KNIGHT: I beseech you pardon me my Lord, if I be mistaken, for my duty cannot be silent, when I think your Highness wrong'd.

LEAR: Thou but rememb'rest me of mine own conception, I have perceived a most faint neglect of late, which I have rather blamed as mine own jealous curiosity than as a very pretence and purpose of unkindness; I will look further into 't: but where's my fool? I have not seen him this two days.

KNIGHT: Since my young Lady's going into France sir, the fool hath much pined away.

LEAR: No more of that, I have noted it well, go you and tell my daughter, I would speak with her. Go you call hither my fool:

Enter Steward.

O you sir, you, come you hither sir, who am I sir?

STEWARD: My Lady's father.

LEAR: My Lady's father? my Lord's knave, you whoreson dog, you slave, you cur.

STEWARD: I am none of these my Lord, I beseech your pardon.

LEAR: Do you bandy looks with me, you rascal?

STEWARD: I'll not be strucken, my Lord.

KENT: Nor tripp'd neither, you base football player.

LEAR: I thank thee fellow. Thou serv'st me, and I'll love thee.

KENT: Come sir, arise, away, I'll teach you differences: away, away, if you will measure your lubber's length again, tarry, but away, go to, have you wisdom, so.

Exit Steward.

LEAR: Now my friendly knave I thank thee; there's earnest of thy service.

Enter Fool.

FOOL: Let me hire him too, here's my coxcomb.

LEAR: How now my pretty knave; how dost thou?

FOOL: Sirrah, you were best take my coxcomb.

LEAR: Why my boy?

FOOL: Why? for taking one's part that's out of favour, nay, and thou canst not smile as the wind sits, thou'lt catch cold shortly, there, take my coxcomb; why this fellow has banish'd two on's daughters, and did the third a blessing against his will; if thou follow him, thou must needs wear my coxcomb. How now, nuncle? Would I had two coxcombs and two daughters.

LEAR: Why my boy?

FOOL: If I gave them all my living, I'ld keep my coxcombs myself, there's mine, beg another of thy daughters.

LEAR: Take heed sirrah, the whip.

FOOL: Truth's a dog must to kennel, he must be whipp'd out, when Lady the Brach may stand by th' fire and stink.

LEAR: A pestilent gall to me.

FOOL: Sirrah, I'll teach thee a speech.

LEAR: Do.

FOOL: Mark it nuncle;

Have more than thou showest,
Speak less than thou knowest,
Lend less than thou owest,
Ride more than thou goest,
Learn more than thou trowest,
Set less than thou throwest;
Leave thy drink and thy whore,
And keep in a door,
And thou shalt have more,
Than two tens to a score.

KENT: This is nothing fool.

FOOL: Then 'tis like the breath of an unfee'd lawyer, you gave me nothing for't, can you make no use of nothing nuncle?

LEAR: Why no, boy, nothing can be made out of nothing.

FOOL: Prithee tell him, so much the rent of his land comes to, he will not believe a fool.

LEAR: A bitter fool.

FOOL: Dost thou know the difference, my boy, between a bitter fool, and a sweet one?

LEAR: No, lad, teach me.

[FOOL: That Lord that counsell'd thee
To give away thy land,
Come place him here by me,
Do thou for him stand;
The sweet and bitter fool
Will presently appear,
The one in motley here,
The other found out there.

LEAR: Dost thou call me fool boy?

FOOL: All thy other titles thou hast given away, that thou wast born with.

KENT: This is not altogether fool my Lord.

FOOL: No faith, Lords and great men will not let me, if I had a monopoly out, they would have part an't, and Ladies too, they will not let me have all fool to myself, they'll be snatching;] give me an egg nuncle, and I'll give thee two crowns.

LEAR: What two crowns shall they be?

FOOL: Why, after I have cut the egg i' th' middle, and eat up the meat, the two crowns of the egg; when thou clovest thy crown i' th' middle, and gav'st away both parts, thou bor'st thine ass on thy back o'er the dirt, thou hadst little wit in thy bald crown, when thou gav'st thy golden one away; if I speak like myself in this, let him be whipp'd that first finds it so.

Fools had ne'er less grace in a year,
For wise men are grown foppish,
They know not how their wits to wear,
Their manners are so apish.

LEAR: When were you wont to be so full of songs, sirrah?

FOOL: I have used it nuncle, e'er since thou mad'st thy daughters thy mothers, for when thou gav'st them the rod, and put'st down thine own breeches,

Then they for sudden joy did weep,
And I for sorrow sung,
That such a King should play bo-peep,
And go the fools among.

Prithee nuncle keep a schoolmaster that can teach thy fool to lie, I would fain learn to lie.

LEAR: An you lie sirrah, we'll have you whipp'd.

FOOL: I marvel what kin thou and thy daughters are, they'll have me whipp'd for speaking true: thou'lt have me whipp'd for lying, and sometimes I am whipp'd for holding my peace. I had rather be any kind o' thing than a fool, and yet I would not be thee nuncle, thou hast pared thy wit o' both sides, and left nothing i' th' middle; here comes one o' the parings.

Enter Goneril.

LEAR: How now daughter? what makes that frontlet on? You are too much of late i' th' frown.

FOOL: Thou wast a pretty fellow when thou hadst no need to care for her frowning, now thou art an O without a figure, I am better than thou art now, I am a fool, thou art nothing. Yes forsooth, I will hold my tongue, so your face bids me, though you say nothing Mum, mum,

He that keeps nor crust, nor crum,
Weary of all, shall want some.

That's a sheal'd peascod.

GONERIL: Not only sir this, your all-licens'd fool,
But other of your insolent retinue
Do hourly carp and quarrel, breaking forth
In rank, and not-to-be-endur'd riots, sir.
I had thought by making this well known unto you,
To have found a safe redress, but now grow fearful
By what yourself too late have spoke and done,
That you protect this course, and put it on
By your allowance, which if you should, the fault

Would not 'scape censure, nor the redresses sleep,
Which in the tender of a wholesome weal,
Might in their working do you that offence,
Which else were shame, that then necessity
Will call discreet proceeding.

FOOL: For you know nuncle,
The hedge-sparrow fed the cuckoo so long,
That it's had it head bit off by it young,
So out went the candle, and we were left darkling.

LEAR: Are you our daughter?

GONERIL: I would you would make use of that good wisdom
(Whereof I know you are fraught) and put away
These dispositions, which of late transport you
From what you rightly are.

FOOL: May not an ass know, when the cart draws the horse?
Whoop Jug I love thee.

LEAR: Does any here know me? This is not Lear:
Does Lear walk thus? Speak thus? Where are his eyes?
Either his notion weakens, his discernings
Are lethargied. Ha! Waking? 'Tis not so?
Who is it that can tell me who I am?

FOOL: Lear's shadow.

[LEAR: I would learn that, for by the marks of sovereignty, knowledge, and reason, I should be false persuaded I had daughters.

FOOL: Which they, will make an obedient father.]

LEAR: Your name, fair gentlewoman?

GONERIL: This admiration sir, is much o' th' savour
Of other your new pranks. I do beseech you
To understand my purposes aright:
As you are old, and reverend, should be wise.
Here do you keep a hundred knights and squires,
Men so disorder'd, so debosh'd, and bold,
That this our Court, infected with their manners,
Shows like a riotous inn; epicurism and lust
Makes it more like a tavern, or a brothel,
Than a grac'd Palace. The shame itself doth speak

For instant remedy. Be then desir'd
By her, that else will take the thing she begs,
A little to disquantity your train,
And the remainders that shall still depend,
To be such men as may besort your age,
Which know themselves, and you.
LEAR: Darkness, and devils.
Saddle my horses: call my train together.
Degenerate bastard, I'll not trouble thee;
Yet have I left a daughter.
GONERIL: You strike my people, and your disorder'd rabble,
Make servants of their betters.
Enter Albany.
LEAR: Woe, that too late repents:
Is it your will, speak, sir? Prepare my horses.
Ingratitude! thou marble-hearted Fiend,
More hideous when thou show'st thee in a child,
Than the sea-monster.
ALBANY: Pray sir be patient.
LEAR: Detested kite, thou liest.
My train are men of choice, and rarest parts,
That all particulars of duty know,
And in the most exact regard, support
The worships of their name. O most small fault,
How ugly didst thou in Cordelia show?
Which like an engine, wrench'd my frame of Nature
From the fix'd place: drew from my heart all love
And added to the gall. O Lear, Lear, Lear!
Beat at this gate that let thy folly in,
And thy dear judgement out. Go, go, my people.
Exeunt Kent and Attendants.
ALBANY: My Lord, I am guiltless, as I am ignorant
Of what hath moved you.
LEAR: It may be so, my Lord.
Hear Nature, hear dear Goddess, hear:
Suspend thy purpose, if thou didst intend

To make this creature fruitful:
Into her womb convey sterility,
Dry up in her the organs of increase,
And from her derogate body never spring
A babe to honour her. If she must teem,
Create her child of spleen, that it may live
And be a thwart disnatur'd torment to her.
Let it stamp wrinkles in her brow of youth,
With cadent tears fret channels in her cheeks,
Turn all her mother's pains and benefits
To laughter and contempt: that she may feel,
How sharper than a serpent's tooth it is,
To have a thankless child. Away, away.

Exit.

ALBANY: Now Gods that we adore, whereof comes this?
GONERIL: Never afflict yourself to know more of it:
But let his disposition have that scope
As dotage gives it.

Enter Lear.

LEAR: What fifty of my followers at a clap?
Within a fortnight?
ALBANY: What's the matter, sir?
LEAR: I'll tell thee; life and death, I am asham'd
That thou hast power to shake my manhood thus,
That these hot tears, which break from me perforce
Should make thee worth them. Blasts and fogs upon thee:
Th' untented woundings of a father's curse
Pierce every sense about thee. Old fond eyes,
Beweep this cause again, I'll pluck ye out,
And cast you with the waters that you lose
To temper clay. Ha? Let it be so.
I have another daughter,
Who I am sure is kind and comfortable:
When she shall hear this of thee, with her nails
She'll flay thy wolvish visage. Thou shalt find,
That I'll resume the shape which thou dost think

I have cast off for ever.

Exit.

GONERIL: Do you mark that?

ALBANY: I cannot be so partial Goneril,
To the great love I bear you.

GONERIL: Pray you content. What Oswald hoa!
You sir, more knave than fool, after your master.

FOOL: Nuncle Lear, nuncle Lear,
Tarry, take the fool with thee:
A fox, when one has caught her,
And such a daughter,
Should sure to the slaughter,
If my cap would buy a halter,
So the fool follows after.

Exit.

GONERIL: This man hath had good counsel, a hundred knights?
'Tis politic, and safe to let him keep
At point a hundred knights: yes, that on every dream,
Each buzz, each fancy, each complaint, dislike,
He may enguard his dotage with their powers,
And hold our lives in mercy. Oswald, I say.

ALBANY: Well, you may fear too far.

GONERIL: Safer than trust too far;
Let me still take away the harms I fear,
Not fear still to be taken. I know his heart,
What he hath utter'd I have writ my sister:
If she sustain him, and his hundred knights
When I have show'd th' unfitness;

Enter Steward.

How now Oswald?
What have you writ that letter to my sister?

OSWALD: Ay Madam.

GONERIL: Take you some company, and away to horse,
Inform her full of my particular fear,
And thereto add such reasons of your own,

As may compact it more. Get you gone,
And hasten your return. (*Exit Oswald.*) No, no, my Lord,
This milky gentleness, and course of yours
Though I condemn not, yet under pardon
You are much more at task for want of wisdom,
Than prais'd for harmful mildness.

ALBANY: How far your eyes may pierce I cannot tell;
Striving to better, oft we mar what's well.

GONERIL: Nay then—

ALBANY: Well, well, th' event.

Exeunt.

I.5

Enter Lear, Kent, Gentleman and Fool.

LEAR: Go you before to Gloucester with these letters; acquaint my daughter no further with any thing you know, than comes from her demand out of the letter; if your diligence be not speedy, I shall be there afore you.

KENT: I will not sleep my Lord, till I have delivered your letter.

Exit.

FOOL: If a man's brains were in's heels, were't not in danger of kibes?

LEAR: Ay boy.

FOOL: Then I prithee be merry, thy wit shall not go slip-shod.

LEAR: Ha, ha, ha.

FOOL: Shalt see thy other daughter will use thee kindly, for though she's as like this, as a crab's like an apple, yet I can tell what I can tell.

LEAR: What canst tell boy?

FOOL: She will taste as like this, as a crab does to a crab: thou canst tell why one's nose stands i' th' middle on's face?

LEAR: No.

FOOL: Why to keep one's eyes of either side's nose, that what a man cannot smell out, he may spy into.

LEAR: I did her wrong.

FOOL: Canst tell how an oyster makes his shell?

LEAR: No.

FOOL: Nor I neither; but I can tell why a snail has a house.

LEAR: Why?

FOOL: Why to put's head in, not to give it away to his daughters, and leave his horns without a case.

LEAR: I will forget my nature, so kind a father? Be my horses ready?

FOOL: Thy asses are gone about 'em; the reason why the seven stars are no more than seven, is a pretty reason.

LEAR: Because they are not eight.

FOOL: Yes indeed, thou wouldst make a good fool.

LEAR: To take't again perforce; Monster Ingratitude!

FOOL: If thou wert my fool nuncle, I'ld have thee beaten for being old before thy time.

LEAR: How's that?

FOOL: Thou shouldst not have been old, till thou hadst been wise.

LEAR: O let me not be mad, not mad sweet heaven:
Keep me in temper, I would not be mad.
How now, are the horses ready?

GENTLEMAN: Ready my Lord.

LEAR: Come boy.

FOOL: She that's a maid now, and laughs at my departure,
Shall not be a maid long, unless things be cut shorter.

Exeunt.

II.1

Enter Bastard and Curan severally.

BASTARD: Save thee Curan.

CURAN: And you sir, I have been with your father, and given him notice that the Duke of Cornwall, and Regan his Duchess will be here with him this night.

BASTARD: How comes that?

CURAN: Nay I know not, you have heard of the news abroad, I mean the whisper'd ones, for they are yet but ear-kissing arguments?

BASTARD: Not I: pray you what are they?

CURAN: Have you heard of no likely wars toward, 'twixt the Dukes of Cornwall, and Albany?

BASTARD: Not a word.

CURAN: You may do then in time, fare you well sir.

Exit.

BASTARD: The Duke be here to-night? The better best,
This weaves itself perforce into my business,
My father hath set guard to take my brother,
And I have one thing of a queasy question
Which I must act; briefness, and fortune work.

Enter Edgar.

Brother, a word, descend; brother I say,
My father watches: O sir, fly this place,
Intelligence is given where you are hid;
You have now the good advantage of the night,
Have you not spoken 'gainst the Duke of Cornwall?
He's coming hither, now, i' th' night, i' th' haste,

And Regan with him, have you nothing said
Upon his party 'gainst the Duke of Albany?
Advise yourself.

EDGAR: I am sure on't, not a word.

BASTARD: I hear my father coming, pardon me:
In cunning, I must draw my sword upon you:
Draw, seem to defend yourself, now quit you well.
Yield, come before my father, light, hoa, here,
Fly brother, torches, torches, so, farewell.

Exit Edgar.

Some blood drawn on me, would beget opinion
Of my more fierce endeavour. I have seen drunkards
Do more than this in sport, eather, father,
Stop, stop, no help?

Enter Gloucester, and Servants with torches.

GLOUCESTER: Now Edmund, where's the villain?

BASTARD: Here stood he in the dark, his sharp sword out,
Mumbling of wicked charms, conjuring the Moon
To stand auspicious mistress.

GLOUCESTER: But where is he?

BASTARD: Look sir, I bleed.

GLOUCESTER: Where is the villain, Edmund?

BASTARD: Fled this way sir, when by no means he could—

GLOUCESTER: Pursue him, ho: go after. By no means, what?

BASTARD: Persuade me to the murther of your Lordship,
But that I told him the revenging Gods,
'Gainst parricides did all the thunder bend,
Spoke with how manifold, and strong a bond
The child was bound to th' father; sir in fine,
Seeing how loathly opposite I stood
To his unnatural purpose, in fell motion
With his prepared sword, he charges home
My unprovided body, latch'd mine arm;
But when he saw my best alarum'd spirits
Bold in the quarrel's right, roused to th' encounter,
Or whether gasted by the noise I made,

Full suddenly he fled.
GLOUCESTER: Let him fly far:
Not in this land shall he remain uncaught,
And found, dispatch; the noble Duke my master,
My worthy arch and patron comes to-night,
By his authority I will proclaim it,
That he which finds him shall deserve our thanks,
Bringing the murderous coward to the stake:
He that conceals him death.
BASTARD: When I dissuaded him from his intent,
And found him pight to do it, with curst speech
I threaten'd to discover him; he replied,
Thou unpossessing bastard, dost thou think,
If I would stand against thee, would the reposal
Of any trust, virtue, or worth in thee
Make thy words faith'd? No, what I should deny,
(As this I would, ay, though thou didst produce
My very character) I'ld turn it all
To thy suggestion, plot, and damned practice:
And thou must make a dullard of the world,
If they not thought the profits of my death
Were very pregnant and potential spirits
To make thee seek it.

Tucket within.

GLOUCESTER: O strange and fastened villain,
Would he deny his letter, said he?
Hark, the Duke's trumpets, I know not why he comes:
All ports I'll bar, the villain shall not 'scape,
The Duke must grant me that: besides, his picture
I will send far and near, that all the kingdom
May have the due note of him, and of my land,
Loyal and natural boy, I'll work the means
To make thee capable.

Enter Cornwall, Regan, and Attendants.

CORNWALL: How now my noble friend, since I came hither,
(Which I can call but now) I have heard strange news.

REGAN: If it be true, all vengeance comes too short
Which can pursue th' offender; how dost my Lord?
GLOUCESTER: O Madam, my old heart is crack'd, its crack'd.
REGAN: What, did my father's godson seek your life?
He whom my father nam'd, your Edgar?
GLOUCESTER: O Lady, Lady, shame would have it hid.
REGAN: Was he not companion with the riotous knights
That tended upon my father?
GLOUCESTER: I know not Madam: 'tis too bad, too bad.
BASTARD: Yes Madam, he was of that consort.
REGAN: No marvel then, though he were ill affected,
'Tis they have put him on the old man's death,
To have th' expense and waste of his revenues:
I have this present evening from my sister
Been well inform'd of them, and with such cautions,
That if they come to sojourn at my house,
I'll not be there.
CORNWALL: Nor I, assure thee Regan.
Edmund, I hear that you have shown your father
A child-like office.
BASTARD: It was my duty sir.
GLOUCESTER: He did bewray his practice; and receive'd
This hurt you see, striving to apprehend him.
CORNWALL: Is he pursued?
GLOUCESTER: Ay my good Lord.
CORNWALL: If he be taken, he shall never more
Be fear'd of doing harm; make your own purpose,
How in my strength you please: for you Edmund,
Whose virtue and obedience doth this instant
So much commend itself, you shall be ours,
Natures of such deep trust, we shall much need:
You we first seize on.
BASTARD: I shall serve you sir truly, however else.
GLOUCESTER: For him I thank your Grace.
CORNWALL: You know not why we came to visit you?
REGAN: Thus out of season, threading dark-ey'd night,

Occasions noble Gloucester of some prize,
Wherein we must have use of your advice.
Our father he hath writ, so hath our sister,
Of differences, which I best thought it fit
To answer from our home: the several messengers
From hence attend dispatch: our good old friend,
Lay comforts to your bosom, and bestow
Your needful counsel to our businesses,
Which craves the instant use.

GLOUCESTER: I serve you Madam,
Your Graces are right welcome.

Exeunt. Flourish.

II.2

Enter Kent and Steward, severally.

STEWARD: Good dawning to thee friend, art of this house?

KENT: Ay.

STEWARD: Where may we set our horses?

KENT: I' th' mire.

STEWARD: Prithee, if thou lov'st me, tell me.

KENT: I love thee not.

STEWARD: Why then I care not for thee.

KENT: If I had thee in Lipsbury pinfold, I would make thee care for me.

STEWARD: Why dost thou use me thus? I know thee not.

KENT: Fellow I know thee.

STEWARD: What dost thou know me for?

KENT: A knave, a rascal, an eater of broken meats, a base, proud, shallow, beggarly, three-suited hundred-pound, filthy worsted-stocking knave, a lily-livered, action-taking, whoreson glass-gazing super-serviceable finical rogue, one trunk-inheriting slave, one that wouldst be a bawd in way of good service, and art nothing but the composition of a knave, beggar, coward, pandar, and the son and heir of a mongrel bitch, one whom I will beat into clamorous whining, if thou deni'st the least syllable of thy addition.

STEWARD: Why, what a monstrous fellow art thou, thus to rail on one, that is neither known of thee, nor knows thee?

KENT: What a brazen-fac'd varlet art thou, to deny thou knowest me? Is it two days ago since I tripp'd up thy heels, and beat thee before the King? Draw you rogue, for though it be night, yet the moon shines, I'll make a sop o' th' moonshine of you, you whoreson cullionly barber-monger, draw.

STEWARD: Away, I have nothing to do with thee.

KENT: Draw you rascal, you come with letters against the King, and take Vanity the puppet's part, against the royalty of her father: draw you rogue, or I'll so carbonado your shanks, draw you rascal, come your ways.

STEWARD: Help, ho, murther, help.

KENT: Strike you slave: stand rogue, stand you neat slave, strike.

STEWARD: Help hoa, murther, murther.

Enter Bastard, Cornwall, Regan, Gloucester, and Servants.

BASTARD: How now, what's the matter? Part.

KENT: With you goodman boy, if you please, come, I'll flesh ye, come on young master.

GLOUCESTER: Weapons? Arms? what's the matter here?

CORNWALL: Keep peace upon your lives, he dies that strikes again, what is the matter?

REGAN: The messengers from our sister, and the King?

CORNWALL: What is your difference, speak?

STEWARD: I am scarce in breath my Lord.

KENT: No marvel, you have so bestirr'd your valour, you cowardly rascal, nature disclaims in thee: a tailor made thee.

CORNWALL: Thou art a strange fellow, a tailor make a man?

KENT: A tailor, sir, a stone-cutter, or a painter, could not have made him so ill, though he had been but two hours o' th' trade.

CORNWALL: Speak yet, how grew your quarrel?

STEWARD: This ancient ruffian sir, whose life I have spar'd at suit of his grey beard.

KENT: Thou whoreson zed, thou unnecessary letter: my Lord, if you will give me leave, I will tread this unbolted villain into mortar, and daub the wall of a jakes with him. Spare my grey beard, you wagtail?

CORNWALL: Peace sirrah,
You beastly knave, know you no reverence?

KENT: Yes sir, but anger hath a privilege.

CORNWALL: Why art thou angry?

KENT: That such a slave as this should wear a sword,
Who wears no honesty: such smiling rogues as these,
Like rats oft bite the holy cords a-twain,
Which are too intrinse t' unloose: smooth every passion
That in the natures of their Lords rebel,
Bring oil to fire, snow to the colder moods,
Renege, affirm, and turn their halcyon beaks
With every gale, and vary of their masters,
Knowing nought (like dogs) but following:
A plague upon your epileptic visage,
Smile you my speeches, as I were a fool?
Goose, if I had you upon Sarum Plain,
I'ld drive ye cackling home to Camelot.

CORNWALL: What art thou mad old fellow?

GLOUCESTER: How fell you out? say that.

KENT: No contraries hold more antipathy,
Than I, and such a knave.

CORNWALL: Why dost thou call him knave?
What is his fault?

KENT: His countenance likes me not.

CORNWALL: No more perchance does mine, nor his, nor hers.

KENT: Sir, 'tis my occupation to be plain,
I have seen better faces in my time,
Than stands on any shoulder that I see
Before me, at this instant.

CORNWALL: This is some fellow,
Who having been prais'd for bluntness, doth affect
A saucy roughness, and constrains the garb
Quite from his Nature. He cannot flatter he,
An honest mind and plain, he must speak truth,
And they will take it so, if not, he's plain.
These kind of knaves I know, which in this plainness
Harbour more craft, and more corrupter ends,
Than twenty silly ducking observants,
That stretch their duties nicely.

KENT: Sir, in good faith, in sincere verity,
Under th' allowance of your great aspect,
Whose influence like the wreath of radiant fire
On flicking Phœbus' front.

CORNWALL: What mean'st by this?

KENT: To go out of my dialect, which you discommend so much; I know sir, I am no flatterer, he that beguil'd you in a plain accent, was a plain knave, which for my part I will not be, though I should win your displeasure to entreat me to 't.

CORNWALL: What was th' offence you gave him?

STEWARD: I never gave him any:
It pleas'd the King his master very late
To strike at me upon his misconstruction,
When he compact, and flattering his displeasure
Tripp'd me behind: being down, insulted, rail'd,
And put upon him such a deal of man,
That worthied him, got praises of the King,
For him attempting, who was self-subdued,
And in the fleshment of this dread exploit,
Drew on me here again.

KENT: None of these rogues, and cowards
But Ajax is their fool.

CORNWALL: Fetch forth the stocks!
You stubborn ancient knave, you reverend braggart,
We'll teach you.

KENT: Sir, I am too old to learn:

Call not your stocks for me, I serve the King,
On whose employment I was sent to you.
You shall do small respects, show too bold malice
Against the grace, and person of my master,
Stocking his messenger.

CORNWALL: Fetch forth the stocks; as I have life and honour,
There shall he sit till noon.

REGAN: Till noon? till night my Lord, and all night too.

KENT: Why Madam, if I were your father's dog,
You should not use me so.

REGAN: Sir, being his knave, I will.

Stocks brought out.

CORNWALL: This is a fellow of the self-same colour,
Our sister speaks of. Come, bring away the stocks.

GLOUCESTER: Let me beseech your Grace, not to do so,
[His fault is much, and] the good King his master
[Will cheque him for't; your purpose'd low correction
Is such, as basest and contemnest wretches
For pilferings and most common trespasses
Are punish'd with;] the King must take it ill,
That he's so slightly valued in his messenger,
Should have him thus restrain'd.

CORNWALL: I'll answer that.

REGAN: My sister may receive it much more worse,
To have her gentleman abus'd, assaulted,
[For following her affairs; put in his legs].

Kent is put in the stocks.

Come my good Lord, away.

Exeunt all but Gloucester and Kent.

GLOUCESTER: I am sorry for thee friend, 'tis the Duke's pleasure,
Whose disposition all the world well knows
Will not be rubb'd nor stopp'd; I'll entreat for thee.

KENT: Pray do not sir, I have watch'd and travell'd hard,
Some time I shall sleep out, the rest I'll whistle:
A good man's fortune may grow out at heels:

Give you good morrow.
GLOUCESTER: The Duke's to blame in this, 'twill be ill taken.
Exit.
KENT: Good King, that must approve the common saw,
Thou out of Heaven's benediction com'st
To the warm sun.
Approach thou beacon to this under globe,
That by thy comfortable beams I may
Peruse this letter. Nothing almost sees miracles
But misery. I know 'tis from Cordelia,
Who hath most fortunately been inform'd
Of my obscured course. And shall find time
From this enormous state, seeking to give
Losses their remedies. All weary and o'er-watch'd,
Take vantage heavy eyes, not to behold
This shameful lodging. Fortune good night,
Smile once more, turn thy wheel.
Enter Edgar.
EDGAR: I heard myself proclaim'd,
And by the happy hollow of a tree,
Escap'd the hunt. No port is free, no place
That guard, and most unusual vigilance
Does not attend my taking. Whiles I may 'scape
I will preserve myself: and am bethought
To take the basest, and most poorest shape
That ever penury in contempt of man,
Brought near to beast; my face I'll grime with filth,
Blanket my loins, elf all my hairs in knots,
And with presented nakedness out-face
The winds, and persecutions of the sky;
The country gives me proof, and precedent
Of Bedlam beggars, who with roaring voices,
Strike in their numb'd and mortified arms,
Pins, wooden-pricks, nails, sprigs of rosemary:
And with this horrible object, from low farms,
Poor pelting villages, sheep-cotes, and mills,

Sometime with lunatic bans, sometime with prayers
Enforce their charity: poor Turlygod, poor Tom,
That's something yet: Edgar I nothing am.

Exit.

Enter Lear, Fool, and Gentleman.

LEAR: 'Tis strange that they should so depart from home,
And not send back my messengers.

GENTLEMAN: As I learn'd,
The night before, there was no purpose in them
Of this remove.

KENT: Hail to thee noble master.

LEAR: Ha? Mak'st thou this shame thy pastime?

KENT: No my Lord.

FOOL: Ha, ha, he wears cruel garters. Horses are tied by the heads, dogs and bears by th' neck, monkeys by th' loins, and men by th' legs: when a man's over-lusty at legs, then he wears wooden nether-stocks.

LEAR: What's he, that hath so much thy place mistook
To set thee here?

KENT: It is both he and she,
Your son, and daughter.

LEAR: No.

KENT: Yes.

LEAR: No I say.

KENT: I say yea.

[LEAR: No no, they would not.

KENT: Yes they have.]

LEAR: By Jupiter I swear no.

KENT: By Juno, I swear ay.

LEAR: They durst not do't:
They could not, would not do't, 'tis worse than murther,
To do upon respect such violent outrage:
Resolve me with all modest haste, which way
Thou mightst deserve, or they impose this usage,
Coming from us.

KENT: My Lord, when at their home

I did commend your Highness' letters to them,
Ere I was risen from the place, that show'd
My duty kneeling, came there a reeking post,
Stew'd in his haste, half breathless, panting forth
From Goneril his mistress, salutations;
Deliver'd letters spite of intermission,
Which presently they read; on those contents,
They summon'd up their meiny, straight took horse,
Commanded me to follow, and attend
The leisure of their answer, gave me cold looks,
And meeting here the other messenger,
Whose welcome I perceiv'd had poison'd mine,
Being the very fellow which of late
Display'd so saucily against your Highness,
Having more man than wit about me, drew;
He rais'd the house, with loud and coward cries,
Your son and daughter found this trespass worth
The shame which here it suffers.

FOOL: Winter's not gone yet, if the wild geese fly that way,
Fathers that wear rags,
Do make their children blind,
But fathers that bear bags,
Shall see their children kind.
Fortune that arrant whore,
Ne'er turns the key to th' poor.
But for all this thou shalt have as many dolours
for thy daughters, as thou canst tell in a year.

LEAR: Oh how this mother swells up toward my heart!
Hysterica passio, down thou climbing sorrow,
Thy element's below; where is this daughter?

KENT: With the Earl sir, here within.

LEAR: Follow me not, stay here.

Exit.

GENTLEMAN: Made you no more offence,
But what you speak of?

KENT: None:

How chance the King comes with so small a number?

FOOL: And thou hadst been set i' th' stocks for that question, thoud'st well deserv'd it.

KENT: Why fool?

FOOL: We'll set thee to school to an ant, to teach thee there's no labouring i' th' winter. All that follow their noses are led by their eyes, but blind men; and there's not a nose among twenty, but can smell him that's stinking; let go thy hold, when a great wheel runs down a hill, lest it break thy neck with following. But the great one that goes upward, let him draw thee after: when a wise man gives thee better counsel, give me mine again; I would have none but knaves follow it, since a fool gives it.

That sir, which serves and seeks for gain,
And follows but for form;
Will pack, when it begins to rain,
And leave thee in the storm.
But I will tarry, the fool will stay,
And let the wise man fly:
The knave turns fool that runs away,
The fool no knave perdy.

Enter Lear with Gloucester.

KENT: Where learn'd you this fool?

FOOL: Not i' th' stocks fool.

LEAR: Deny to speak with me?
They are sick, they are weary,
They have travell'd all the night? mere fetches,
The images of revolt and flying off.
Fetch me a better answer.

GLOUCESTER: My dear Lord,
You know the fiery quality of the Duke,
How unremoveable and fix'd he is
In his own course.

LEAR: Vengeance, plague, death, confusion:
Fiery? what quality? Why Gloucester, Gloucester,
I'ld speak with the Duke of Cornwall, and his wife.

GLOUCESTER: Well my good Lord, I have inform'd them so.

LEAR: Inform'd them? Dost thou understand me man.

GLOUCESTER: Ay my good Lord.

LEAR: The King would speak with Cornwall,
The dear father
Would with his daughter speak, commands, tends, service,
Are they inform'd of this? My breath and blood:
Fiery? The fiery Duke, tell the hot Duke that—
No, but not yet, may be he is not well,
Infirmity doth still neglect all office,
Whereto our health is bound, we are not ourselves,
When Nature being oppress'd, commands the mind
To suffer with the body; I'll forbear,
And am fall'n out with my more headier will,
To take the indispos'd and sickly fit,
For the sound man. Death on my state: wherefore
Should he sit here? This act persuades me,
That this remotion of the Duke and her
Is practice only. Give me my servant forth;
Go tell the duke and's wife, I'ld speak with them:
Now, presently: bid them come forth and hear me,
Or at their chamber-door I'll beat the drum,
Till it cry sleep to death.

GLOUCESTER: I would have all well betwixt you.

Exit.

LEAR: Oh me my heart! My rising heart! But down.

FOOL: Cry to it nuncle, as the cockney did to the eels, when she put 'em i' th' paste alive, she knapp'd 'em o' th' coxcombs with a stick, and cried down wantons, down; 'twas her brother, that in pure kindness to his horse buttered his hay.

Enter Cornwall, Regan, Gloucester, and Servants.

LEAR: Good morrow to you both.

CORNWALL: Hail to your Grace.

Kent here set at liberty.

REGAN: I am glad to see your Highness.

LEAR: Regan, I think you are. I know what reason

I have to think so, if thou shouldst not be glad,
I would divorce me from thy mother's tomb,
Sepulchring an adultress. O are you free?
Some other time for that. Beloved Regan,
Thy sister's naught: O Regan, she hath tied
Sharp-tooth'd unkindness, like a vulture here,
I can scarce speak to thee, thou'lt not believe
With how deprav'd a quality. O Regan.

REGAN: I pray you sir, take patience, I have hope
You less know how to value her desert,
Than she to scant her duty.

LEAR: Say? How is that?

REGAN: I cannot think my sister in the least
Would fail her obligation. If sir perchance
She have restrained the riots of your followers,
'Tis on such ground, and to such wholesome end,
As clears her from all blame.

LEAR: My curses on her.

REGAN: O sir, you are old,
Nature in you stands on the very verge
Of her confine: you should be rul'd, and led
By some discretion, that discerns your state
Better than you yourself: therefore I pray you,
That to our sister, you do make return,
Say you have wrong'd her.

LEAR: Ask her forgiveness?
Do you but mark how this becomes the house?
Dear daughter, I confess that I am old;
Age is unnecessary: on my knees I beg,
That you'll vouchsafe me raiment, bed, and food.

REGAN: Good sir, no more; these are unsightly tricks;
Return you to my sister.

LEAR: Never Regan:
She hath abated me of half my train;
Look'd black upon me, struck me with her tongue
Most serpent-like, upon the very heart.

All the stor'd Vengeances of Heaven fall
On her ingrateful top: strike her young bones
You taking airs, with lameness.
CORNWALL: Fie, sir, fie.
LEAR: You nimble lightnings, dart your blinding flames
Into her scornful eyes: infect her beauty,
You fen-suck'd fogs, drawn by the powerful sun,
To fall, and blister.
REGAN: O the blest Gods! so will you wish on me,
When the rash mood is on.
LEAR: No Regan, thou shalt never have my curse:
Thy tender-hefted Nature shall not give
Thee o'er to harshness: her eyes are fierce, but thine
Do comfort, and not burn. 'Tis not in thee
To grudge my pleasures, to cut off my train,
To bandy hasty words, to scant my sizes,
And in conclusion, to oppose the bolt
Against my coming in. Thou better know'st
The offices of Nature, bond of childhood,
Effects of courtesy, dues of gratitude:
Thy half o' th' Kingdom hast thou not forgot,
Wherein I thee endow'd.
REGAN: Good sir, to th' purpose.
Tucket within.
LEAR: Who put my man i' th' stocks?
Enter Steward.
CORNWALL: What trumpet's that?
REGAN: I know't, my sister's: this approves her letter,
That she would soon be here.
Is your lady come?
LEAR: This is a slave, whose easy-borrowed pride
Dwells in the sickly grace of her he follows.
Out varlet, from my sight.
CORNWALL: What means your Grace?
Enter Goneril.
LEAR: Who stock'd my servant? Regan, I have good hope
Thou didst not know on't. Who comes here? O Heavens!

If you do love old men; if your sweet sway
Allow obedience; if yourselves are old,
Make it your cause: send down, and take my part.
Art not asham'd to look upon this beard?
O Regan, will you take her by the hand?
GONERIL: Why not by th' hand, sir? How have I offended?
All's not offence that indiscretion finds,
And dotage terms so.
LEAR: O sides, you are too tough!
Will you yet hold? How came my man i' th' stocks?
CORNWALL: I sent him there, sir: but his own disorders
Deserv'd much less advancement.
LEAR: You? Did you?
REGAN: I pray you father being weak, seem so.
If till the expiration of your month
You will return and sojourn with my sister,
Dismissing half your train, come then to me,
I am now from home, and out of that provision
Which shall be needful for your entertainment.
LEAR: Return to her? and fifty men dismiss'd?
No, rather I abjure all roofs, and choose
To wage against the enmity o' th' air,
To be a comrade with the wolf, and owl,
Necessity's sharp pinch. Return with her?
Why the hot-blooded France, that dowerless took
Our youngest born, I could as well be brought
To knee his throne, and squire-like pension beg,
To keep base life afoot; return with her?
Persuade me rather to be slave and sumpter
To this detested groom.
GONERIL: At your choice sir.
LEAR: I prithee daughter do not make me mad,
I will not trouble thee my child: farewell:
We'll no more meet, no more see one another.
But yet thou art my flesh, my blood, my daughter,
Or rather a disease that's in my flesh,

Which I must needs call mine. Thou art a boil,
A plague sore, or imbossed carbuncle
In my corrupted blood. But I'll not chide thee,
Let shame come when it will, I do not call it,
I do not bid the Thunder-bearer shoot,
Nor tell tales of thee to high-judging Jove.
Mend when thou canst, be better at thy leisure,
I can be patient, I can stay with Regan,
I and my hundred knights.
REGAN: Not altogether so,
I look'd not for you yet, nor am provided
For your fit welcome, give ear sir to my sister,
For those that mingle reason with your passion,
Must be content to think you old, and so,
But she knows what she does.
LEAR: Is this well spoken?
REGAN: I dare avouch it sir, what fifty followers?
Is it not well? What should you need of more?
Yes, or so many? Sith that both charge and danger,
Speak 'gainst so great a number? How in one house
Should many people, under two commands
Hold amity? 'Tis hard, almost impossible.
GONERIL: Why might not you my Lord, receive attendance
From those that she calls servants, or from mine?
REGAN: Why not my Lord? If then they chanc'd to slack ye,
We could control them; If you will come to me,
(For now I spy a danger) I entreat you
To bring but five and twenty, to no more
Will I give place or notice.
LEAR: I gave you all.
REGAN: And in good time you gave it.
LEAR: Made you my guardians, my depositaries,
But kept a reservation to be follow'd
With such a number. What, must I come to you
With five and twenty? Regan said you so?
REGAN: And speak't again my Lord, no more with me.

LEAR: Those wicked creatures yet do look well-favour'd
When others are more wicked, not being the worst
Stands in some rank of praise, I'll go with thee,
Thy fifty yet doth double five-and-twenty,
And thou art twice her love.
GONERIL: Hear me my Lord;
What need you five and twenty? Ten? Or five?
To follow in a house, where twice so many
Have a command to tend you?
REGAN: What need one?
LEAR: O reason not the need: our basest beggars
Are in the poorest thing superfluous,
Allow not Nature, more than Nature needs:
Man's life is as cheap as beast's. Thou art a Lady;
If only to go warm were gorgeous,
Why Nature needs not what thou gorgeous wear'st,
Which scarcely keeps thee warm, but for true need,
You Heavens, give me that patience, patience I need,
You see me here, you Gods, a poor old man,
As full of grief as age, wretched in both,
If it be you that stirs these daughters' hearts
Against their father, fool me not so much,
To bear it tamely: touch me with noble anger,
And let not women's weapons, water-drops,
Stain my man's cheeks. No you unnatural hags,
I will have such revenges on you both,
That all the world shall—I will do such things,
What they are yet, I know not, but they shall be
The terrors of the earth! You think I'll weep,
No, I'll not weep. I have full cause of weeping.
Storm and Tempest.
But this heart shall break into a hundred thousand flaws
Or ere I'll weep: O fool, I shall go mad.
Exit, with his followers and Gloucester.
CORNWALL: Let us withdraw, 'twill be a storm.
REGAN: This house is little, the old man and's his people,

Cannot be well bestow'd.
GONERIL: 'Tis his own blame hath put himself from rest,
And must needs taste his folly.
REGAN: For his particular, I'll receive him gladly,
But not one follower.
GONERIL: So am I purpos'd.
Where is my Lord of Gloucester?

Enter Gloucester.

CORNWALL: Follow'd the old man forth, he is return'd.
GLOUCESTER: The King is in high rage.
CORNWALL: Whither is he going?
GLOUCESTER: He calls to horse, but will I know not whither.
CORNWALL: 'Tis best to give him way, he leads himself.
GONERIL: My Lord, entreat him by no means to stay.
GLOUCESTER: Alack the night comes on, and the high winds
Do sorely ruffle, for many miles about
There's scarce a bush.
REGAN: O sir, to wilful men,
The injuries that they themselves procure,
Must be their schoolmasters: shut up your doors,
He is attended with a desperate train,
And what they may incense him to, being apt,
To have his ear abus'd, wisdom bids fear.
CORNWALL: Shut up your doors my Lord; 'tis a wild night,
My Regan counsels well: come out o' th' storm.

Exeunt.

III.1

Storm still. Enter Kent and a Gentleman, severally.

KENT: Who's there besides foul weather?
GENTLEMAN: One minded like the weather, most unquietly.

KENT: I know you: where's the King?
GENTLEMAN: Contending with the fretful elements;
Bids the wind blow the earth into the sea,
Or swell the curled waters 'bove the main,
That things might change, or cease; [tears his white hair,
Which the impetuous blasts with eyeless rage
Catch in their fury, and make nothing of;
Strives in his little world of man to out-scorn
The to-and-fro-conflicting wind and rain;
This night wherein the cub-drawn bear would couch,
The lion, and the belly-pinched wolf
Keep their fur dry, unbonneted he runs,
And bids what will take all.]
KENT: But who is with him?
GENTLEMAN: None but the fool, who labours to out-jest
His heart-struck injuries.
KENT: Sir, I do know you,
And dare upon the warrant of my note
Commend a dear thing to you. There is division
(Although as yet the face of it cover'd
With mutual cunning,) 'twixt Albany, and Cornwall:
Who have, as who have not, that their great stars
Throne'd and set high, servants, who seem no less,
Which are to France the spies and speculations,
Intelligent of our state. What hath been seen,
Either in snuffs, and packings of the Dukes,
Or the hard rein which both of them have borne
Against the old kind king; or something deeper,
Whereof (perchance) these are but furnishings;
[But true it is, from France there comes a power
Into this scatter'd Kingdom, who already
Wise in our negligence have secret feet
In some of our best ports, and are at point
To show their open banner. Now to you,
If on my credit you dare build so far,
To make your speed to Dover, you shall find

Some that will thank you, making just report
Of how unnatural and bemadding sorrow
The King hath cause to plain.
I am a gentleman of blood and breeding,
And from some knowledge and assurance, offer
This office to you.]

GENTLEMAN: I will talk further with you.

KENT: No, do not:
For confirmation that I am much more
Than my out-wall, open this purse, and take
What it contains. If you shall see Cordelia,
(As fear not but you shall) show her this ring,
And she will tell you who that fellow is
That yet you do not know. Fie on this storm,
I will go seek the King.

GENTLEMAN: Give me your hand, have you no more to say?

KENT: Few words, but to effect more than all yet;
That when we have found the King, in which your pain
That way, I'll this: he that first lights on him,
Holla the other.

Exeunt.

III.2

Storm still.
Enter Lear, and Fool.

LEAR: Blow winds, and crack your cheeks; rage, blow
You cataracts and hurricanoes spout,
Till you have drench'd our steeples, drown'd the cocks.
You sulphurous and thought-executing fires,
Vaunt-couriers to oak-cleaving thunderbolts,
Singe my white head. And thou all-shaking thunder,

Strike flat the thick rotundity o' th' world,
Crack Nature's moulds, all germens spill at once
That makes ingrateful man.

FOOL: O nuncle, Court holy-water in a dry house, is better than this rain-water out o' door. Good nuncle, in, ask thy daughters' blessing: here's a night pities neither wise men, nor fools.

LEAR: Rumble thy bellyful: spit fire, spout rain:
Nor rain, wind, thunder, fire are my daughters;
I tax not you, you elements with unkindness.
I never gave you Kingdom, call'd you children;
You owe me no subscription. Then let fall
Your horrible pleasure. Here I stand your slave,
A poor, infirm, weak, and despise'd old man:
But yet I call you servile ministers,
That will with two pernicious daughters join
Your high-engender'd battles, 'gainst a head
So old, and white as this. O, ho! 'tis foul.

FOOL: He that has a house to put's head in, has a good head-piece:

The cod-piece that will house,
Before the head has any;
The head, and he shall louse:
So beggars marry many.
The man that makes his toe,
What he his heart should make,
Shall of a corn cry woe,
And turn his sleep to wake.

For there was never yet fair woman, but she made mouths in a glass.

Enter Kent.

LEAR: No, I will be the pattern of all patience,
I will say nothing.

KENT: Who's there?

FOOL: Marry here's Grace and a cod-piece; that's a wise man, and a fool.

KENT: Alas sir are you here? Things that love night,

Love not such nights as these: the wrathful skies
Gallow the very wanderers of the dark
And make them keep their caves: since I was man,
Such sheets of fire, such bursts of horrid thunder,
Such groans of roaring wind, and rain, I never
Remember to have heard. Man's Nature cannot carry
Th' affliction, nor the fear.

LEAR: Let the great Gods
That keep this dreadful podder o'er our heads,
Find out their enemies now. Tremble thou wretch,
That hast within thee undivulged crimes
Unwhipp'd of Justice. Hide thee, thou bloody hand;
Thou perjur'd, and thou simular man of virtue
That art incestuous. Caitiff, to pieces shake
That under covert, and convenient seeming
Hast practis'd on man's life. Close pent-up guilts,
Rive your concealing continents, and cry
These dreadful summoners grace. I am a man,
More sinn'd against, than sinning.

KENT: Alack, bare-headed?
Gracious my Lord, hard by here is a hovel,
Some friendship will it lend you 'gainst the tempest:
Repose you there, while I to this hard house,
(More harder than the stones whereof 'tis rais'd,
Which even but now, demanding after you,
Deni'd me to come in) return, and force
Their scanted courtesy.

LEAR: My wits begin to turn.
Come on my boy. How dost my boy? Art cold?
I am cold myself. Where is this straw, my fellow?
The art of our necessities is strange,
And can make vile things precious. Come, your hovel
Poor fool, and knave, I have one part in my heart
That's sorry yet for thee.

FOOL: He that has and a little tiny wit,
With heigh-ho, the wind and the rain,

Must make content with his fortunes fit,
Though the rain it raineth every day.
LEAR: True boy: come, bring us to this hovel.

Exeunt Lear and Kent.

FOOL: This is a brave night to cool a courtezan;
I'll speak a prophecy ere I go:
When priests are more in word, than matter;
When brewers mar their malt with water;
When nobles are their tailors' tutors,
No heretics burn'd, but wenches' suitors;
When every case in Law, is right;
No squire in debt, nor no poor knight;
When slanders do not live in tongues;
Nor cutpurses come not to throngs;
When usurers tell their gold i' th' field,
And bawds, and whores, do churches build,
Then shall the Realm of Albion,
Come to great confusion:
Then comes the time, who lives to see't,
That going shall be us'd with feet.
This prophecy Merlin shall make, for I live before his time.

Exit.

III.3

Enter Gloucester, and Bastard.

GLOUCESTER: Alack, alack Edmund, I like not this unnatural dealing, when I desired their leave that I might pity him, they took from me the use of mine own house, charg'd me on pain of their perpetual displeasure, neither to speak of him, entreat for him, nor any way sustain him.

BASTARD: Most savage and unnatural.

GLOUCESTER: Go to; say you nothing. There is a division betwixt the Dukes, and a worse matter than that: I have received a letter this night, 'tis dangerous to be spoken, I have lock'd the letter in my closet, these injuries the King now bears, will be revenged home; there is part of a power already footed, we must incline to the King, I will look him, and privily relieve him; go you and maintain talk with the Duke, that my charity be not of him perceived; if he ask for me, I am ill, and gone to bed; if I die for it (as no less is threatened me, the King my old master must be relieved. There is some strange things toward Edmund, pray you be careful.

Exit.

BASTARD: This courtesy forbid thee, shall the Duke
Instantly know, and of that letter too;
This seems a fair deserving, and must draw me
That which my father loses: no less than all;
The younger rises, when the old doth fall.

Exit.

III.4

Enter Lear, Kent, and Fool.

KENT: Here is the place my Lord, good my Lord enter,
The tyranny of the open night's too rough
For Nature to endure.

Storm still.

LEAR: Let me alone.

KENT: Good my Lord enter here.

LEAR: Wilt break my heart?

KENT: I had rather break mine own, good my Lord enter.

LEAR: Thou think'st 'tis much that this contentious storm
Invades us to the skin: so 'tis to thee,

But where the greater malady is fix'd,
The lesser is scarce felt. Thou 'ldst shun a bear,
But if thy flight lay toward the raging sea,
Thou 'ldst meet the bear i' th' mouth; when the mind's free,
The body's delicate: the tempest in my mind,
Doth from my senses take all feeling else,
Save what beats there, filial ingratitude,
Is it not as this mouth should tear this hand
For lifting food to't? But I will punish home;
No, I will weep no more; In such a night,
To shut me out? Pour on, I will endure:
In such a night as this? O Regan, Goneril,
Your old kind father, whose frank heart gave all,
O that way madness lies, let me shun that:
No more of that.

KENT: Good my Lord enter here.

LEAR: Prithee go in thyself, seek thine own ease,
This tempest will not give me leave to ponder
On things would hurt me more; But I'll go in,
In boy, go first. You houseless poverty;

Exit Fool.

Nay, get thee in; I'll pray and then I'll sleep.
Poor naked wretches, whereso'er you are
That bide the pelting of this pitiless storm,
How shall your houseless heads, and unfed sides,
Your loop'd, and window'd raggedness defend you
From such seasons as these? O I have ta'en
Too little care of this: take physic, Pomp,
Expose thyself to feel what wretches feel,
That thou mayst shake the superflux to them,
And show the Heavens more just.

Enter Edgar and Fool.

EDGAR: Fathom, and half, fathom and half: poor Tom.

FOOL: Come not in here nuncle, here's a spirit, help me, help me.

KENT: Give me thy hand, who's there?

FOOL: A spirit, a spirit, he says his name's poor Tom.

KENT: What art thou that dost grumble there i' the straw? Come forth.

EDGAR: Away, the foul fiend follows me, through the sharp hawthorn blow the winds. Hum, go to thy bed, and warm thee.

LEAR: Didst thou give all to thy daughters? And art thou come to this?

EDGAR: Who gives any thing to poor Tom? Whom the foul fiend hath led through fire, and through flame, through sword, and whirlpool, o'er bog, and quagmire, that hath laid knives under his pillow, and halters in his pew, set ratsbane by his porridge, made film proud of heart, to ride on a bay trotting horse, over four-inched bridges, to course his own shadow for a traitor. Bless thy five wits, Tom's a-cold. O do de, do, de, do de, bless thee from whirlwinds, star-blasting, and taking, do poor Tom some charity, whom the foul Fiend vexes. There could I have him now, and there, and there again, and there.

Storm still.

LEAR: Has his daughters brought him to this pass?
Couldst thou save nothing? Wouldst thou give 'em all?

FOOL: Nay, he reserv'd a blanket, else we had been all sham'd.

LEAR: Now all the plagues that in the pendulous air
Hang fated o'er men's faults, light on thy daughters.

KENT: He hath no daughters sir.

LEAR: Death traitor, nothing could have subdued Nature
To such a lowness, but his unkind daughters.
Is it the fashion, that discarded fathers,
Should have thus little mercy on their flesh:
Judicious punishment, 'twas this flesh begot
Those pelican daughters.

EDGAR: Pillicock sat on Pillicock-hill,
Alow, alow, loo, loo.

FOOL: This cold night will turn us all to fools, and madmen.

EDGAR: Take heed o' the foul Fiend, obey thy parents, keep thy words Justice, swear not, commit not with man's sworn spouse; set not thy sweet heart on proud array. Tom's a-cold.

LEAR: What hast thou been?

EDGAR: A serving-man! Proud in heart, and mind; that curl'd my hair, wore gloves in my cap; serv'd the lust of my mistress' heart, and did the act of darkness with her. Swore as many oaths, as I spake words, and broke them in' the sweet face of Heaven. One, that slept in the contriving of lust, and wak'd to do it. Wine lov'd I dearly, dice dearly; and in woman, out-paramour'd the Turk. False of heart, light of ear, bloody of hand; hog in sloth, fox in stealth, wolf in greediness, dog in madness, lion in prey. Let not the creaking of shoes, nor the rustling of silks, betray thy poor heart to woman. Keep thy foot out of brothels, thy hand out of plackets, thy pen from lenders' books, and defy the foul Fiend. Still through the hawthorn blows the cold wind: says suum, mun, nonny, Dolphin my boy, Boy Sesey: let him trot by.

Storm still.

LEAR: Thou wert better in a grave, than to answer with thy uncover'd body, this extremity of the skies. Is man no more than this? Consider him well. Thou ow'st the worm no silk; the beast, no hide; the sheep, no wool; the cat, no perfume. Ha? here's three on's are sophisticated. Thou art the thing itself; unaccommodated man, is no more but such a poor, bare, forked animal as thou art. Off, off you lendings: come, unbutton here.

Enter Gloucester, with a torch.

FOOL: Prithee nuncle be contented, 'tis a naughty night to swim in. Now a little fire in a wild field, were like an old lecher's heart, a small spark, all the rest on's body, cold: look, here comes a walking fire.

EDGAR: This is the foul fiend Flibbertigibbet; he begins at curfew, and walks till the first cock: he gives the web and the pin, squints the eye, and makes the hare-lip; mildews the white wheat, and hurts the poor creature of earth.
Swithhold footed thrice the old,
He met the Night-mare, and her nine-fold;
Bid her alight, and her troth plight,

And, aroint thee witch, aroint thee.
KENT: How fares your Grace?
LEAR: What's he?
KENT: Who's there? What is't you seek?
GLOUCESTER: What are you there? Your names?
EDGAR: Poor Tom, that eats the swimming frog, the toad, the tadpole, the wall-newt, and the water: that in the fury of his heart, when the foul Fiend rages, eats cow-dung for sallets; swallows the old rat, and the ditch-dog; drinks the green mantle of the standing pool: who is whipp'd from tithing to tithing, and stock'd, punish'd, and imprison'd: who hath had three suits to his back, six shirts to his body:

Horse to ride, and weapon to wear:
But mice, and rats, and such small deer,
Have been Tom's food, for seven long year:
Beware my follower. Peace Smulkin, peace thou Fiend.

GLOUCESTER: What, hath your grace no better company?
EDGAR: The Prince of Darkness is a gentleman. Modo he's call'd, and Mahu.
GLOUCESTER: Our flesh and blood, my Lord, that is grown so vile, it doth hate what gets it.
EDGAR: Poor Tom's a-cold.
GLOUCESTER: Go in with me; my duty cannot suffer
T' obey in all your daughters' hard commands:
Though their injunction be to bar my doors,
And let this tyrannous night take hold upon you,
Yet have I ventured to come seek you out,
And bring you where both fire, and food is ready.
LEAR: First let me talk with this philosopher,
What is the cause of thunder?
KENT: Good my Lord take his offer, go into th' house.
LEAR: I'll talk a word with this same learned Theban:
What is your study?
EDGAR: How to prevent the Fiend, and to kill vermin.
LEAR: Let me ask you one word in private.
KENT: Importune him once more to go my Lord,
His wits begin t' unsettle.

GLOUCESTER: Canst thou blame him?
Storm still.
His daughters seek his death: ah, that good Kent,
He said it would be thus: poor banish'd man:
Thou say'st the King grows mad, I'll tell thee friend
I am almost mad myself. I had a son,
Now outlaw'd from my blood: he sought my life
But lately: very late: I lov'd him, friend,
No father his son dearer: truth to tell thee,
The grief hath craz'd my wits. What a night's this?
I do beseech your Grace.
LEAR: O cry your mercy, sir:
Noble philosopher, your company.
EDGAR: Tom's a-cold.
GLOUCESTER: In fellow there, into th' hovel; keep thee warm.
LEAR: Come, let's in all.
KENT: This way, my Lord.
LEAR: With him; I will keep still with my philosopher.
KENT: Good my Lord, soothe him: let him take the fellow.
GLOUCESTER: Take him you on.
KENT: Sirrah, come on; go along with us.
LEAR: Come, good Athenian.
GLOUCESTER: No words, no words, hush.
EDGAR: Child Rowland to the dark Tower came,
His word was still, fie, foh, and fum,
I smell the blood of a British man.
Exeunt.

III.5

Enter Cornwall, and Bastard.

CORNWALL: I will have my revenge, ere I depart his house.
BASTARD: How my Lord, I may be censured, that Nature thus gives way to Loyalty, something fears me to think of.

CORNWALL: I now perceive, it was not altogether your brother's evil disposition made him seek his death: but a provoking merit set a-work by a reproveable badness in himself.

BASTARD: How malicious is my fortune, that I must repent to be just? This is the letter which he spoke of; which approves him an intelligent party to the advantages of France. O Heavens! that this treason were not; or not I the detector.

CORNWALL: Go with me to the Duchess.

BASTARD: If the matter of this paper be certain, you have mighty business in hand.

CORNWALL: True or false, it hath made thee Earl of Gloucester: seek out where thy father is, that he may be ready for our apprehension.

BASTARD: If I find him comforting the King, it will stuff his suspicion more fully. I will persevere in my course of loyalty, though the conflict be sore between that, and my blood.

CORNWALL: I will lay trust upon thee; and thou shalt find a dear father in my love.

Exeunt.

III.6

Enter Kent and Gloucester.

GLOUCESTER: Here is better than the open air, take it thankfully: I will piece out the comfort with what addition I can: I will not be long from you.

Exit.

KENT: All the power of his wits, have given way to his impatience: the Gods reward your kindness.

Enter Lear, Edgar and Fool.

EDGAR: Frateretto calls me, and tells me Nero is an angler in the lake of Darkness: pray innocent, and beware the foul Fiend.

FOOL: Prithee nuncle tell me, whether a madman be a gentleman, or a yeoman.

LEAR: A King, a King.

FOOL: No, he's a yeoman, that has a gentleman to his son: for he's a mad yeoman that sees his son a gentleman before him.

LEAR: To have a thousand with red burning spits
Come hizzing in upon 'em.

[EDGAR: The foul fiend bites my back.

FOOL: He's mad, that trusts in the tameness of a wolf, a horse's health, a boy's love, or a whore's oath.

LEAR: It shall be done, I will arraign them straight;
Come sit thou here most learned justice,
Thou sapient sir sit here, no you she foxes—

EDGAR: Look where he stands and glares, want'st thou eyes, at tria madam?
Come o'er the bourn Bessy to me.

FOOL: Her boat hath a leak,
And she must not speak,
Why she dares not come, over to thee.

EDGAR: The foul Fiend haunts poor Tom in the voice of a nightingale, Hopdance cries in Tom's belly for two white herring, croak not black angel, I have no food for thee.

KENT: How do you sir? Stand you not so amaz'd,
Will you lie down and rest upon the cushions?

LEAR: I'll see their trial first. Bring in their evidence.
Thou robed man of justice take thy place,
And thou his yoke-fellow of equity,
Bench by his side; you are o' th' commission,
Sit you too.

EDGAR: Let us deal justly.
Sleepest or wakest thou, jolly shepherd,
Thy sheep be in the corn,
And for one blast of thy minikin mouth,
Thy sheep shall take no harm.

Pur the cat is gray.

LEAR: Arraign her first, 'tis Goneril. I here take my oath before this honourable assembly, she kicked the poor King her father.

FOOL: Come hither mistress, is your name Goneril?

LEAR: She cannot deny it.

FOOL: Cry you mercy, I took you for a joint-stool.

LEAR: And here's another, whose warp'd looks proclaim
What store her heart is made on; stop her there,
Arms, arms, sword, fire, corruption in the place,
False justicer why hast thou let her 'scape?]

EDGAR: Bless thy five wits.

KENT: O pity: sir, where is the patience now
That thou so oft have boasted to retain?

EDGAR: My tears begin to take his part so much,
They mar my counterfeiting.

LEAR: The little dogs, and all;
Tray, Blanch, and Sweet-heart: see, they bark at me.

EDGAR: Tom, will throw his head at them:
Avaunt you curs,
Be thy mouth or black or white:
Tooth that poisons if it bite:
Mastiff, greyhound, mongrel, grim,
Hound or spaniel, brach or lym:
Or bobtail tike, or trundle-tail,
Tom will make them weep and wail,
For with throwing thus my head,
Dogs leap the hatch, and all are fled.

Do, de, de, de: sesse: come, march to wakes and fairs, and market-towns: poor Tom thy horn is dry.

LEAR: Then let them anatomize Regan: see what breeds about her heart. Is there any cause in Nature that makes these hard-hearts? You sir, I entertain for one of my hundred; only, I do not like the fashion of your garments. You will say they are Persian; but let them be chang'd.

Enter Gloucester.

KENT: Now good my Lord, lie here, and rest awhile.

LEAR: Make no noise, make no noise, draw the curtains: so, so, we'll go to supper i' th' morning.

FOOL: And I'll go to bed at noon.

GLOUCESTER: Come hither friend: where is the King my master?

KENT: Here sir, but trouble him not, his wits are gone.

GLOUCESTER: Good friend, I prithee take him in thy arms;
I have o'erheard a plot of death upon him:
There is a litter ready, lay him in't,
And drive toward Dover friend, where thou shalt meet
Both welcome, and protection. Take up thy master,
If thou shouldst dally half an hour, his life
With thine, and all that offer to defend him,
Stand in assured loss. Take up, take up,
And follow me, that will to some provision
Give thee quick conduct.

[KENT: Oppressed nature sleeps:
This rest might yet have balm'd thy broken sinews,
Which if convenience will not allow,
Stand in hard cure. Come, help to bear thy master,
Thou must not stay behind.]

GLOUCESTER: Come, come away.

Exeunt all but Edgar.

[EDGAR: When we our betters see bearing our woes,
We scarcely think our miseries our foes.
Who alone suffers, suffers most i' th' mind,
Leaving free things and happy shows behind,
But then the mind much sufferance doth o'erskip,
When grief hath mates, and bearing fellowship:
How light and portable my pain seems now,
When that which makes me bend, makes the King bow,
He childed as I father'd, Tom, away.
Mark the high noises; and thyself bewray,
When false opinion, whose wrong thoughts defile thee,
In thy just proof, repeals and reconciles thee:
What will hap more to-night, safe 'scape the King,
Lurk, lurk.

Exit.]

III.7

Enter Cornwall, Regan, Goneril, Bastard, and Servants.

CORNWALL: Post speedily to my Lord your husband, show him this letter, the army of France is landed: seek out the traitor Gloucester.

Exit a Servants.

REGAN: Hang him instantly.

GONERIL: Pluck out his eyes.

CORNWALL: Leave him to my displeasure. Edmund, keep you our sister company: the revenges we are bound to take upon your traitorous father, are not fit for your beholding. Advise the Duke where you are going, to a most festinate preparation: we are bound to the like. Our posts shall be swift, and intelligent betwixt us. Farewell dear sister, farewell my Lord of Gloucester.

Enter Steward.

How now? Where's the King?

STEWARD: My Lord of Gloucester hath convey'd him hence:
Some five or six and thirty of his knights
Hot questrists after him, met him at gate,
Who, with some other of the Lords, dependants,
Are gone with him toward Dover: where they boast to have well-armed friends.

CORNWALL: Get horses for your mistress.

GONERIL: Farewell sweet Lord, and sister.

Exeunt Goneril, Bastard and Steward.

CORNWALL: Edmund farewell: go seek the traitor Gloucester,
Pinion him like a thief, bring him before us:
Though well we may not pass upon his life
Without the form of justice, yet our power
Shall do a courtesy to our wrath, which men
May blame, but not control.

Enter Gloucester and Servants.

Who's there? The traitor?
REGAN: Ingrateful fox, 'tis he.
CORNWALL: Bind fast his corky arms.
GLOUCESTER: What mean your Graces? Good my friends consider
Your are my guests: do me no foul play, friends.
CORNWALL: Bind him I say.
REGAN: Hard, hard: O filthy traitor.
GLOUCESTER: Unmerciful Lady as you are, I'm none.
CORNWALL: To this chair bind him, villain, thou shalt find—
GLOUCESTER: By the kind Gods, 'tis most ignobly done
To pluck me by the beard.
REGAN: So white, and such a traitor?
GLOUCESTER: Naughty Lady,
These hairs which thou dost ravish from my chin
Will quicken and accuse thee. I am your host,
With robbers' hands, my hospitable favours
You should not ruffle thus. What will you do?
CORNWALL: Come sir,
What letters had you late from France?
REGAN: Be simple answer'd, for we know the truth.
CORNWALL: And what confederacy have you with the traitors, late footed in the Kingdom?
REGAN: To whose hands have you sent the lunatic King: Speak.
GLOUCESTER: I have a letter guessingly set down
Which came from one that's of a neutral heart,
And not from one oppos'd.
CORNWALL: Cunning.
REGAN: And false.
CORNWALL: Where hast thou sent the King?
GLOUCESTER: To Dover.
REGAN: Wherefore to Dover? Wast thou not charg'd at peril?
CORNWALL: Wherefore to Dover? Let him first answer that.

GLOUCESTER: I am tied to th' stake, and I must stand the course.
REGAN: Wherefore to Dover?
GLOUCESTER: Because I would not see thy cruel nails
Pluck out his poor old eyes: nor thy fierce sister,
In his anointed flesh, stick boarish fangs.
The sea, with such a storm as his bare head,
In hell-black night indur'd, would have buoy'd up
And quench'd the stelled fires:
Yet poor old heart, he holp the Heavens to rain.
If wolves had at thy gate howl'd that stern time,
Thou shouldst have said, good porter turn the key:
All cruels else subscribe: but I shall see
The winged vengeance overtake such children.
CORNWALL: See't shalt thou never. Fellows hold the chair.
Upon these eyes of thine, I'll set my foot.
GLOUCESTER: He that will think to live, till he be old,
Give me some help.—O cruel! O you Gods.
REGAN: One side will mock another: th' other too.
CORNWALL: If you see vengeance.
FIRST SERVANT: Hold your hand, my Lord:
I have serv'd you ever since I was a child:
But better service have I never done you,
Than now to bid you hold.
REGAN: How now, you dog?
FIRST SERVANT: If you did wear a beard upon your chin, I'd shake it on this quarrel. What do you mean?
CORNWALL: My villain?

They draw and fight.

FIRST SERVANT: Nay then come on, and take the chance of anger.
REGAN: Give me thy sword. A peasant stand up thus?

She takes a sword, and runs at him behind.

FIRST SERVANT: Oh I am slain: My Lord, you have one eye left
To see some mischief on him. Oh.

Dies.

CORNWALLL: Lest it see more, prevent it; out vile jelly:
Where is thy lustre now?
GLOUCESTER: All dark and comfortless?
Where's my son Edmund?
Edmund, enkindle all the sparks of Nature
To quit this horrid act.
REGAN: Out treacherous villain,
Thou call'st on him, that hates thee. It was he
That made the overture of thy treasons to us:
Who is too good to pity thee.
GLOUCESTER: O my follies! then Edgar was abus'd;
Kind Gods, forgive me that, and prosper him.
REGAN: Go thrust him out at gates, and let him smell
His way to Dover.

Exit one with Gloucester.

How is't my Lord? How look you?
CORNWALL: I have receiv'd a hurt: follow me Lady;
Turn out that eyeless villain: throw this slave
Upon the dunghill: Regan, I bleed apace,
Untimely comes this hurt. Give me your arm.

Exeunt.

[SECOND SERVANT: I'll never care what wickedness I do,
If this man come to good.
THIRD SERVANT: If she live long.
And in the end meet the old course of death,
Women will all turn monsters.
SECOND SERVANT: Let's follow the old Earl, and get the Bedlam
To lead him where he would: his roguish madness
Allows itself to any thing.
THIRD SERVANT: Go thou: I'll fetch some flax and whites of eggs
To apply to his bleeding face. Now heaven help him.

Exeunt.]

IV.1

Enter Edgar.

EDGAR: Yet better thus, and known to be contemn'd,
Than still contemn'd and flatter'd, to be worst:
The lowest and most dejected thing of Fortune,
Stands still in esperance, lives not in fear:
The lamentable change is from the best,
The worst returns to laughter. Welcome then,
Thou unsubstantial air that I embrace:
The wretch that thou hast blown unto the worst,
Owes nothing to thy blasts.

Enter Gloucester, and an Old Man.

But who comes here? My father poorly led?
World, world, O world!
But that thy strange mutations make us hate thee,
Life would not yield to age.

OLD MAN: O my good Lord, I have been your tenant, and your father's tenant, these fourscore years.

GLOUCESTER: Away, get thee away: good friend be gone,
Thy comforts can do me no good at all,
Thee, they may hurt.

OLD MAN: You cannot see your way.

GLOUCESTER: I have no way, and therefore want no eyes:
I stumbled when I saw. Full oft 'tis seen,
Our means secure us, and our mere defects
Prove our commodities. O dear son Edgar,
The food of thy abused father's wrath:
Might I but live to see thee in my touch,
I'ld say I had eyes again.

OLD MAN: How now? who's there?

EDGAR: O Gods! Who is't can say I am at the worst?
I am worse than e'er I was.
OLD MAN: 'Tis poor mad Tom.
EDGAR: And worse I may be yet: the worst is not,
So long as we can say this is the worst.
OLD MAN: Fellow, where goest?
GLOUCESTER: Is it a beggar-man?
OLD MAN: Madman, and beggar too.
GLOUCESTER: He has some reason, else he could not beg.
I' th' last night's storm, I such a fellow saw;
Which made me think a man, a worm. My son
Came then into my mind, and yet my mind
Was then scarce friends with him.
I have heard more since:
As flies to wanton boys, are we to the Gods,
They kill us for their sport.
EDGAR: How should this be?
Bad is the trade that must play fool to sorrow,
Angering itself, and others. Bless thee master.
GLOUCESTER: Is that the naked fellow?
OLD MAN: Ay, my Lord.
GLOUCESTER: Get thee away: if for my sake
Thou wilt o'ertake us hence a mile or twain
I' th' way toward Dover, do it for ancient love,
And bring some covering for this naked soul,
Which I'll entreat to lead me.
OLD MAN: Alack sir, he is mad.
GLOUCESTER: 'Tis the times' plague, when madmen lead the blind:
Do as I bid thee, or rather do thy pleasure:
Above the rest, be gone.
OLD MAN: I'll bring him the best 'parel that I have,
Come on't, what will.

Exit.

GLOUCESTER: Sirrah, naked fellow.
EDGAR: Poor Tom's a-cold. I cannot daub it further.
GLOUCESTER: Come hither fellow.

EDGAR: And yet I must:
Bless thy sweet eyes, they bleed.

GLOUCESTER: Know'st thou the way to Dover?

EDGAR: Both stile, and gate; horse-way, and foot-path: poor Tom hath been scar'd out of his good wits. Bless thee good man's son, from the foul Fiend. [Five fiends have been in poor Tom at once; of lust, as Obidicut, Hobbididance Prince of dumbness, Mahu of stealing, Modo of murder, Flibbertigibbet of mopping and mowing who since possesses chambermaids and waiting-women, so, bless thee, master.]

GLOUCESTER: Here take this purse, thou whom the heavens' plagues
Have humbled to all strokes: that I am wretched
Makes thee happier: Heavens deal so still:
Let the superfluous, and lust-dieted man,
That slaves your ordinance, that will not see
Because he does not feel, feel your power quickly:
So distribution should undo excess,
And each man have enough, Dost thou know Dover?

EDGAR: Ay master.

GLOUCESTER: There is a cliff, whose high and bending head
Looks fearfully in the confined deep:
Bring me but to the very brim of it,
And I'll repair the misery thou dost bear
With something rich about me: from that place
I shall no leading need.

EDGAR: Give me thy arm;
Poor Tom shall lead thee.

Exeunt.

IV.2

Enter Goneril, Bastard, and Steward.

GONERIL: Welcome my Lord. I marvel our mild husband
Not met us on the way. Now, where's your master?
STEWARD: Madam within, but never man so chang'd:
I told him of the army that was landed:
He smil'd at it. I told him you were coming,
His answer was, the worse. Of Gloucester's treachery,
And of the loyal service of his son
When I inform'd him, then he call'd me sot.
And told me I had turn'd the wrong side out:
What most he should dislike, seems pleasant to him;
What like, offensive.
GONERIL: Then shall you go no further.
It is the cowish terror of his spirit
That dares not undertake: he'll not feel wrongs
Which tie him to an answer. our wishes on the way
May prove effects. Back, Edmund to my brother,
Hasten his musters, and conduct his powers.
I must change names at home, and give the distaff
Into my husband's hands. This trusty servant
Shall pass between us: ere long you are like to hear
(If you dare venture in your own behalf)
A mistress's command. Wear this; spare speech,
Decline your head. This kiss, if it durst speak
Would stretch thy spirits up into the air:
Conceive, and fare thee well.
BASTARD: Yours in the ranks of death.
Exit.
GONERIL: My most dear Gloucester.

Oh, the difference of man, and man,
To thee a woman's services are due,
My fool usurps my body.
STEWARD: Madam, here comes my Lord.
Exit.
Enter Albany.
GONERIL: I have been worth the whistle.
ALBANY: O Goneril,
You are not worth the dust which the rude wind
Blows in your face. [I fear your disposition:
That nature which contemns i' th' origin
Cannot be border'd certain in itself;
She that herself will sliver and disbranch
From her material sap, perforce must wither,
And come to deadly use.
GONERIL: No more, the text is foolish.
ALBANY: Wisdom and goodness, to the vile seem vile,
Filths savour but themselves, what have you done?
Tigers, not daughters, what have you perform'd?
A father, and a gracious aged man
Whose reverence even the head-lugg'd bear would lick,
Most barbarous, most degenerate have you madded.
Could my good brother suffer you to do it?
A man, a Prince, by him so benefited,
If that the heavens do not their visible spirits
Send quickly down to tame this vile offences,
It will come,
Humanity must perforce prey on itself.
Like monsters of the deep.]
GONERIL: Milk-liver'd man,
That bear'st a cheek for blows, a head for wrongs,
Who hast not in thy brows an eye discerning
Thine honour, from thy suffering; [that not know'st,
Fools do those villains pity who are punish'd
Ere they have done their mischief, Where's thy drum?
France spreads his banners in our noiseless land,

With plumed helm, thy state begins to threat:
Whilst thou a moral fool sit'st still and cries,
Alack why does he so?]

ALBANY: See thyself devil:
Proper deformity seems not in the Fiend
So horrid as in woman.

GONERIL: O vain fool.

[ALBANY: Thou changed, and self-cover'd thing for shame
Be-monster not thy feature, were't my fitness
To let these hands obey my blood,
They are apt enough to dislocate and tear
Thy flesh and bones, howe'er thou art a fiend,
A woman's shape doth shield thee.

GONERIL: Marry your manhood now—]

Enter a Messenger.

[ALBANY: What news?]

MESSENGER: O my good Lord, the Duke of Cornwall's dead,
Slain by his servant, going to put out
The other eye of Gloucester.

ALBANY: Gloucester's eyes.

MESSENGER: A servant that he bred, thrill'd with remorse,
Oppos'd against the act: bending his sword
To his great master, who, thereat enrag'd,
Flew on him, and amongst them fell'd him dead,
But not without that harmful stroke, which since
Hath pluck'd him after.

ALBANY: This shows you are above
You justices, that these our nether crimes
So speedily can venge. But (O poor Gloucester)
Lost he his other eye?

MESSENGER: Both, both, my Lord.
This letter Madam, craves a speedy answer:
'Tis from your sister.

GONERIL: One way I like this well.
But being widow, and my Gloucester with her,
May all the building in my fancy pluck

Upon my hateful life. Another way
The news is not so tart. I'll read, and answer.

Exit.

ALBANY: Where was his son, when they did take his eyes?

MESSENGER: Come with my Lady hither.

ALBANY: He is not here.

MESSENGER: No my good Lord, I met him back again.

ALBANY: Knows he the wickedness?

MESSENGER: Ay my good Lord: 'twas he inform'd against him.
And quit the house on purpose, that their punishment
Might have the freer course.

ALBANY: Gloucester, I live
To thank thee for the love thou show'dst the King,
And to revenge thine eyes. Come hither friend,
Tell me what more thou know'st.

Exeunt.

[IV.3

Enter Kent and a Gentleman.

KENT: Why the King of France is so suddenly gone back, know you no reason?

GENTLEMAN: Something he left imperfect in the state, which since his coming forth is thought of, which imports to the Kingdom, so much fear and danger that his personal return was most required and necessary.

KENT: Who hath he left behind him, General?

GENTLEMAN: The Marshal of France Monsieur La Far.

KENT: Did your letters pierce the Queen to any demonstration of grief?

GENTLEMAN: I say she took them, read them in my presence,
And now and then an ample tear trill'd down

Her delicate cheek, it seem'd she was a Queen
Over her passion, who most rebel-like,
Sought to be King o'er her.

KENT: O then it moved her.

GENTLEMAN: Not to a rage, patience and sorrow strove
Who should express her goodliest, you have seen
Sunshine and rain at once, her smiles and tears,
Were like a better way: those happy smilets,
That play'd on her ripe lip seem'd not to know,
What guests were in her eyes which parted thence,
As pearls from diamonds dropp'd; in brief,
Sorrow would be a rarity most beloved,
If all could so become it.

KENT: Made she no verbal question?

GENTLEMAN: 'Faith once or twice she heav'd the name of father,
Pantingly forth as if it press'd her heart,
Cried sisters, sisters, shame of Ladies, sisters:
Kent, father, sisters, what, i' th' storm i' th' night;
Let pity not be believ'd, there she shook
The holy water from her heavenly eyes,
And clamour moisten'd her; then away she started,
To deal with grief alone.

KENT: It is the stars,
The stars above us govern our conditions,
Else one self mate and mate could not beget,
Such different issues. You spoke not with her since?

GENTLEMAN: No.

KENT: Was this before the King return'd?

GENTLEMAN: No, since.

KENT: Well sir, the poor distressed Lear's i' th' town,
Who sometime in his better tune remembers,
What we are come about, and by no means
Will yield to see his daughter.

GENTLEMAN: Why good sir?

KENT: A sovereign shame so elbows him; his own unkindness

That stripp'd her from his benediction, turn'd her,
To foreign casualties, gave her dear rights
To his dog-hearted daughters, these things sting
His mind, so venomously that burning shame
Detains him from Cordelia.

GENTLEMAN: Alack poor gentleman.

KENT: Of Albany's and Cornwall's powers you heard not?

GENTLEMAN: 'Tis so they are afoot.

KENT: Well sir, I'll bring you to our master Lear,
And leave you to attend him: some dear cause
Will in concealment wrap me up awhile;
When I am known aright you shall not grieve,
Lending me this acquaintance. I pray you go
Along with me.

Exeunt.]

IV.4

Enter with drum and colours, Cordelia, Gentleman and Soldiers.

CORDELIA: Alack, 'tis he: why he was met even now
As mad as the vex'd sea, singing aloud,
Crown'd with rank fumiter and furrow-weeds,
With bur-docks, hemlock, nettles, cuckoo-flowers,
Darnel, and all the idle weeds that grow
In our sustaining corn. A century send forth;
Search every acre in the high-grown field,
And bring him to our eye. What can man's wisdom
In the restoring his bereaved sense?
He that helps him, take all my outward worth.

GENTLEMAN: There is means, Madam:
Our foster-nurse of Nature, is repose,

The which he lacks: that to provoke in him
Are many simples operative, whose power
Will close the eye of anguish.
CORDELIA: All blest secrets,
All you unpublish'd virtues of the earth
Spring with my tears; be aidant, and remediate
In the good man's distress: seek, seek for him,
Lest his ungovern'd rage, dissolve the life
That wants the means to lead it.

Enter Messenger.

MESSENGER: News Madam,
The British powers are marching hitherward.
CORDELIA: 'Tis known before. Our preparation stands
In expectation of them. O dear father,
It is thy business that I go about: therefore great France
My mourning, and importune tears hath pitied:
No blown ambition doth our arms incite,
But love, dear love, and our ag'd father's right:
Soon may I hear, and see him.

Exeunt.

IV.5

Enter Regan and Steward.

REGAN: But are my brother's powers set forth?
STEWARD: Ay Madam.
REGAN: Himself in person there?
STEWARD: Madam with much ado:
Your sister is the better soldier.
REGAN: Lord Edmund spake not with your Lord at home?
STEWARD: No Madam.
REGAN: What might import my sister's letter to him?
STEWARD: I know not, Lady.

REGAN: 'Faith he is posted hence on serious matter:
It was great ignorance, Gloucester's eyes being out
To let him live. Where he arrives, he moves
All hearts against us: Edmund, I think is gone
In pity of his misery, to dispatch
His nighted life: moreover to descry
The strength o' th' enemy.
STEWARD: I must needs after him, Madam, with my letter.
REGAN: Our troops set forth to-morrow, stay with us:
The ways are dangerous.
STEWARD: I may not Madam:
My Lady charg'd my duty in this business.
REGAN: Why should she write to Edmund? Might not you
Transport her purposes by word? Belike,
Some things, I know not what. I'll love thee much
Let me unseal the letter.
STEWARD: Madam, I had rather—
REGAN: I know your Lady does not love her husband,
I am sure of that: and at her late being here,
She gave strange œillades, and most speaking locks
To noble Edmund. I know you are of her bosom.
STEWARD: I, Madam?
REGAN: I speak in understanding: you are: I know't;
Therefore I do advise you take this note:
My Lord is dead: Edmund, and I have talk'd,
And more convenient is he for my hand
Than for your Lady's: you may gather more:
If you do find him, pray you give him this;
And when your mistress hears thus much from you,
I pray desire her call her wisdom to her.
So fare you well:
If you do chance to hear of that blind traitor,
Preferment falls on him, that cuts him off.
STEWARD: Would I could meet him Madam, I should show
What party I do follow.
REGAN: Fare thee well.

Exeunt.

IV.6

Enter Gloucester, and Edgar.

GLOUCESTER: When shall I come to th' top of that same hill?
EDGAR: You do climb up it now. Look how we labour.
GLOUCESTER: Methinks the ground is even.
EDGAR: Horrible steep.
Hark, do you hear the sea?
GLOUCESTER: No truly.
EDGAR: Why then your other senses grow imperfect
By your eyes' anguish.
GLOUCESTER: So may it be indeed.
Methinks thy voice is alter'd, and thou speak'st
In better phrase, and matter than thou didst.
EDGAR: You are much deceiv'd: in nothing am I chang'd
But in my garments.
GLOUCESTER: Methinks you are better spoken.
EDGAR: Come on sir, here's the place: stand still; how fearful
And dizzy 'tis, to cast one's eyes so low,
The crows and choughs, that wing the midway air
Show scarce so gross as beetles. Half way down
Hangs one that gathers samphire: dreadful trade:
Methinks he seems no bigger than his head.
The fishermen, that walk'd upon the beach
Appear like mice; and yond tall anchoring bark,
Diminish'd to her cock; her cock, a buoy
Almost too small for sight. The murmuring surge,
That on th' unnumber'd idle pebbles chafes
Cannot be heard so high. I'll look no more,
Lest my brain turn, and the deficient sight
Topple down headlong.

GLOUCESTER: Set me where you stand.
EDGAR: Give me your hand:
  You are now within a foot of th' extreme verge:
  For all beneath the moon would I not leap upright.
GLOUCESTER: Let go my hand:
  Here friend's another purse: in it, a jewel
  Well worth a poor man's taking. Fairies, and Gods
  Prosper it with thee. Go thou further off,
  Bid me farewell, and let me hear thee going.
EDGAR: Now fare you well, good sir.
GLOUCESTER: With all my heart.
EDGAR: Why I do trifle thus with his despair,
  Is done to cure it.

He kneels.

GLOUCESTER: O you mighty Gods!
  This world I do renounce, and in your sights
  Shake patiently my great affliction off:
  If I could bear it longer, and not fall
  To quarrel with your great opposeless wills,
  My snuff, and loathed part of Nature should
  Burn itself out. If Edgar live, O bless him:
  Now fellow, fare thee well.

He falls.

EDGAR: Gone sir, farewell:
  And yet I know not how conceit may rob
  The treasury of life, when life itself
  Yields to the theft. Had he been where he thought,
  By this had thought been past. Alive, or dead?
  Hoa, you sir: friend hear you sir, speak:
  Thus might he pass indeed: yet he revives.
  What are you sir?
GLOUCESTER: Away, and let me die.
EDGAR: Hadst thou been aught but gossamer, feathers, air,
  (So many fathom down precipitating)
  Thou'dst shiver'd like an egg: but thou dost breathe:
  Hast heavy substance, bleed'st not, speak'st, art sound.

Ten masts at each, make not the altitude
Which thou hast perpendicularly fell,
Thy life's a miracle. Speak yet again.
GLOUCESTER: But have I fall'n, or no?
EDGAR: From the dread summit of this chalky bourn.
Look up a height; the shrill-gorg'd lark so far
Cannot be seen, or heard: do but look up.
GLOUCESTER: Alack, I have no eyes:
Is wretchedness depriv'd that benefit
To end itself by death? 'Twas yet some comfort,
When misery could beguile the tyrant's rage,
And frustrate his proud will.
EDGAR: Give me your arm.
Up, so: how is 't? Feel you your legs? You stand.
GLOUCESTER: Too well, too well.
EDGAR: This is above all strangeness.
Upon the crown o' th' cliff, what thing was that
Which parted from you?
GLOUCESTER: A poor unfortunate beggar.
EDGAR: As I stood here below, methought his eyes
Were two full moons: he had a thousand noses,
Horns whelk'd, and waved like the enraged sea:
It was some Fiend: therefore thou happy father,
Think that the clearest Gods, who make them honours
Of men's impossibilities, have preserved thee.
GLOUCESTER: I do remember now: henceforth I'll bear
Affliction, till it do cry out itself
Enough, enough, and die. That thing you speak of,
I took it for a man: often 'twould say
The Fiend, the Fiend; he led me to that place.
EDGAR: Bear free and patient thoughts.

Enter Lear, mad.

But who comes here?
The safer sense will ne'er accommodate
His master thus.

LEAR: No, they cannot touch me for coining. I am the King himself.

EDGAR: O thou side-piercing sight!

LEAR: Nature's above Art, in that respect. There's your press-money. That fellow handles his bow, like a crow-keeper: draw me a clothier's yard. Look, look, a mouse: peace, peace, this piece of toasted cheese will do't. There's my gauntlet, I'll prove it on a giant. Bring up the brown bills. O well flown bird: i' th' clout, i' th' clout: hewgh. Give the word.

EDGAR: Sweet marjoram.

LEAR: Pass.

GLOUCESTER: I know that voice.

LEAR: Ha! Goneril with a white beard! They flatter'd me like a dog, and told me I had white hairs in my beard, ere the black ones were there. To say ay, and no, to every thing that I said: ay, and no too, was no good divinity. When the rain came to wet me once, and the wind to make me chatter: when the thunder would not peace at my bidding, there I found 'em, there I smelt 'em out. Go to, they are not men o' their words; they told me, I was every thing: 'tis a lie, I am not ague-proof.

GLOUCESTER: The trick of that voice, I do well remember: Is't not the King?

LEAR: Ay, every inch a King: When I do stare, see how the subject quakes. I pardon that man's life. What was thy cause? Adultery? Thou shalt not die: die for adultery? No, the wren goes to't, and the small gilded fly does lecher in my sight. Let copulation thrive: for Gloucester's bastard son was kinder to his father, than my daughters got 'tween the lawful sheets. To't Luxury pell-mell, for I lack soldiers. Behold yond simpering dame, whose face between her forks presages snow; that minces virtue, and does shake the head to hear of pleasure's name, the fitchew, nor the soiled horse goes to't with a more riotous appetite. Down from the waist they are Centaurs, though women all above: but to the girdle do the gods inherit, beneath is all the Fiends. There's hell, there's darkness, there's the sulphurous pit; burning, scalding, stench, consumption; fie, fie; fie; pah, pah: give me an ounce of civet; good apothecary sweeten my imagination: there's money for thee.

GLOUCESTER: O let me kiss that hand.

LEAR: Let me wipe it first, it smells of mortality.

GLOUCESTER: O ruin'd piece of Nature, this great world
Shall so wear out to nought. Dost thou know me?

LEAR: I remember thine eyes well enough: dost thou squiny at me? No, do thy worst blind Cupid! I'll not love. Read thou this challenge, mark but thy penning of it.

GLOUCESTER: Were all thy letters suns, I could not see.

EDGAR: I would not take this from report, it is,
And my heart breaks at it.

LEAR: Read.

GLOUCESTER: What with the case of eyes?

LEAR: Oh ho, are you there with me? No eyes in your head, nor no money in your purse? Your eyes are in a heavy case, your purse in a light, yet you see how this world goes.

GLOUCESTER: I see it feelingly.

LEAR: What, art mad? A man may see how this world goes, with no eyes. Look with thine ears: see how yond Justice rails upon yond simple thief. Hark in thine ear: change places, and handy-dandy, which is the Justice, which is the thief: thou hast seen a farmer's dog bark at a beggar?

GLOUCESTER: Ay sir.

LEAR: And the creature run from the cur: there thou mightst behold the great image of authority: a dog's obey'd in office. Thou, rascal beadle, hold thy bloody hand: why dost thou lash that whore? Strip thy own back, thou hotly lust'st to use her in that kind, for which thou whipp'st her. The usurer hangs the cozener. Through rough tatter'd clothes great vices do appear: robes, and furr'd gowns hide all. Plate sins with gold, and the strong lance of Justice, hurtless breaks: arm it in rags, a pigmy's straw does pierce it. None does offend, none, I say none, I'll able 'em; take that of me my friend, who have the power to seal th' accuser's lips. Get thee glass-eyes, and like a scurvy politician, seem to see the things thou dost not. Now, now, now, now. Pull off my boots: harder, harder, so.

EDGAR: O matter, and impertinency mix'd,
Reason in madness.
LEAR: If thou wilt weep my fortunes, take my eyes.
I know thee well enough, thy name is Gloucester:
Thou must be patient; we came crying hither:
Thou know'st, the first time that we smell the air
We wawl, and cry. I will preach to thee: mark.
GLOUCESTER: Alack, alack the day.
LEAR: When we are born, we cry that we are come
To this great stage of fools. This's a good block:
It were a delicate stratagem to shoe
A troop of horse with felt: I'll put't in proof,
And when I have stol'n upon these sons-in-law,
Then kill, kill, kill, kill, kill, kill.
Enter a Gentleman.
GENTLEMAN: O here he is: lay hand upon him, sir.
Your most dear daughter—
LEAR: No rescue? What, a prisoner? I am even
The natural fool of Fortune. Use me well,
You shall have ransom. Let me have surgeons,
I am cut to th' brains.
GENTLEMAN: You shall have any thing.
LEAR: No seconds? All myself?
Why, this would make a man, a man of salt
To use his eyes for garden water-pots,
[Ay and laying autumn's dust.]
I will die bravely, like a smug bridegroom. What?
I will be jovial: come, come, I am a King,
My masters, know you that?
GENTLEMAN: You are a royal one, and we obey you.
LEAR: Then there's life in't. Come, and you get it, you shall get it running: sa, sa, sa, sa.
Exit Lear running.
GENTLEMAN: A sight most pitiful in the meanest wretch,
Past speaking of in a King. Thou hast a daughter
Who redeems Nature from the general curse

Which twain have brought her to.
EDGAR: Hail gentle sir.
GENTLEMAN: Sir, speed you: what's your will?
EDGAR: Do you hear aught, sir, of a battle toward?
GENTLEMAN: Most sure, and vulgar: every one hears that,
Which can distinguish sound.
EDGAR: But by your favour;
How near's the other army?
GENTLEMAN: Near, and on speedy foot: the main descry
Stands on the hourly thought.
EDGAR: I thank you sir, that's all.
GENTLEMAN: Though that the Queen on special cause is here,
Her army is mov'd on.
EDGAR: I thank you sir.

Exit Gentleman.

GLOUCESTER: You ever-gentle Gods, take my breath from me,
Let not my worser spirit tempt me again
To die before you please.
EDGAR: Well pray you father.
GLOUCESTER: Now good sir, what are you?
EDGAR: A most poor man, made tame to Fortune's blows
Who, by the art of known, and feeling sorrows,
Am pregnant to good pity. Give me your hand,
I'll lead you to some biding.
GLOUCESTER: Hearty thanks:
The bounty, and the benison of Heaven
To boot, and boot.

Enter Steward.

STEWARD: A proclaim'd prize: most happy
That eyeless head of thine, was first fram'd flesh
To raise my fortunes. Thou old, unhappy traitor,
Briefly thy self remember: the sword is out
That must destroy thee.
GLOUCESTER: Now let thy friendly hand
Put strength enough to't.
STEWARD: Wherefore, bold peasant,

Dar'st thou support a publish'd traitor? Hence,
Lest that th' infection of his fortune take
Like hold on thee. Let go his arm.

EDGAR: Chill not let go zir, without vurther 'casion.

STEWARD: Let go slave, or thou diest.

EDGAR: Good gentleman go your gait, and let poor volk pass: and 'chud ha' bin zwagger'd out of my life, 'twould not ha' bin zo long as 'tis, by a vortnight. Nay, come not near th' old man: keep out che vor' ye, or ise try whether your costard, or my ballow be the harder; chill be plain with you.

STEWARD: Out dunghill.

They fight.

EDGAR: Chill pick your teeth zir: come, no matter vor your foins.

STEWARD: Slave thou hast slain me: villain, take my purse;
If ever thou wilt thrive, bury my body,
And give the letters which thou find'st about me,
To Edmund Earl of Gloucester: seek him out
Upon the English party. O untimely death, death.

Dies.

EDGAR: I know thee well. A serviceable villain,
As duteous to the vices of thy Mistress,
As badness would desire.

GLOUCESTER: What, is he dead?

EDGAR: Sit you down father: rest you.
Let's see these pockets; the letters that he speaks of
May be my friends: he's dead; I am only sorry
He had no other death's-man. Let us see:
Leave gentle wax, and manners, blame us not.
To know our enemies' minds, we rip their hearts,
Their papers is more lawful.

Reads the letter.

Let our reciprocal vows be remember'd. You have many opportunities to cut him off: if your will want not, time and place will be fruitfully offer'd. There is nothing done. If he return the conqueror, then am I the prisoner, and his bed, my

gaol, from the loathed warmth whereof, deliver me, and supply the place for your labour.
Your (wife, so I would say)
Affectionate servant,
GONERIL

O undistinguish'd space of woman's will,
A plot upon her virtuous husband's life,
And the exchange my brother: here in the sands,
Thee I'll rake up, the post unsanctified
Of murderous lechers: and in the mature time,
With this ungracious paper strike the sight
Of the death-practis'd Duke: for him 'tis well,
That of thy death, and business, I can tell.
GLOUCESTER: The King is mad: how stiff is my vile sense
That I stand up, and have ingenious feeling
Of my huge sorrows? Better I were distract,
So should my thoughts be sever'd from my griefs,
Drum afar off.
And woes, by wrong imaginations lose
The knowledge of themselves.
EDGAR: Give me your hand:
Far off methinks I heard the beaten drum.
Come father, I'll bestow you with a friend.
Exeunt.

IV.7

Enter Cordelia, Kent, and Doctor.

CORDELIA: O thou good Kent, how shall I live and work
To match thy goodness? My life will be too short,
And every measure fail me
KENT: To be acknowledg'd, Madam is o'erpaid,

All my reports go with the modest truth,
Nor more, nor clipp'd, but so.
CORDELIA: Be better suited;
These weeds are memories of those worser hours;
I prithee put them off.
KENT: Pardon dear Madam,
Yet to be known shortens my made intent,
My boon I make it, that you know me not,
Till time and I, think meet.
CORDELIA: Then be 't so my good Lord: how does the King?
DOCTOR: Madam sleeps still.
CORDELIA: O you kind Gods!
Cure this great breach in his abused Nature,
Th' untun'd and jarring senses, O wind up,
Of this child-changed father.
DOCTOR: So please your Majesty,
That we may wake the King, he hath slept long.
CORDELIA: Be govern'd by your knowledge, and proceed I' th'
sway of your own will: is he array'd?

Enter Lear in a chair carried by servants.

DOCTOR: Ay Madam: in the heaviness of sleep,
We put fresh garments on him.
Be by good Madam when we do awake him,
I doubt of his temperance.
[CORDELIA: Very well.
DOCTOR: Please you draw near, louder the music there.]
CORDELIA: O my dear father, restoration hang
Thy medicine on my lips, and let this kiss
Repair those violent harms, that my two sisters
Have in thy reverence made.
KENT: Kind and dear Princess.
CORDELIA: Had you not been their father, these white flakes
Had challenge pity of them. Was this a face
To be oppos'd against the jarring winds?
[To stand against the deep dread-bolted thunder?
In the most terrible and nimble stroke
Of quick cross lightning, to watch *poor perdu*
With this thin helm?] Mine enemy's dog,

Though he had bit me, should have stood that night
Against my fire, and wast thou fain, poor father,
To hovel thee with swine and rogues forlorn,
In short, and musty straw? Alack, alack,
'Tis wonder that thy life and wits, at once
Had not concluded all. He wakes, speak to him.

DOCTOR: Madam do you, 'tis fittest.

CORDELIA: How does my royal Lord? How fares your Majesty?

LEAR: You do me wrong to take me out o' th' grave,
Thou art a soul in bliss, but I am bound
Upon a wheel of fire, that mine own tears
Do scald, like molten lead.

CORDELIA: Sir, do you know me?

LEAR: You are a spirit I know, when did you die?

CORDELIA: Still, still, far wide.

DOCTOR: He's scarce awake, let him alone awhile.

LEAR: Where have I been? Where am I? Fair daylight?
I am mightily abus'd; I should e'en die with pity.
To see another thus. I know not what to say:
I will not swear these are my hands: let's see,
I feel this pin prick, would I were assur'd
Of my condition.

CORDELIA: O look upon me sir,
And hold your hand in benediction o'er me,
You must not kneel.

LEAR: Pray do not mock me:
I am a very foolish fond old man,
Fourscore and upward, not an hour more, nor less:
And to deal plainly,
I fear I am not in my perfect mind.
Methinks I should know you, and know this man,
Yet I am doubtful: for I am mainly ignorant
What place this is: and all the skill I have
Remembers not these garments: nor I know not
Where I did lodge last night. Do not laugh at me,
For, as I am a man, I think this Lady
To be my child Cordelia.

CORDELIA: And so I am: I am.

LEAR: Be your tears wet? yes, 'faith: I pray weep not:
If you have poison for me, I will drink it:
I know you do not love me, for your sisters
Have, as I do remember, done me wrong.
You have some cause, they have not.

CORDELIA: No cause, no cause.

LEAR: Am I in France?

KENT: In your own kingdom sir.

LEAR: Do not abuse me.

DOCTOR: Be comforted good Madam, the great rage
You see is kill'd in him: [and yet it is danger
To make him even o'er the time he has lost:]
Desire him to go in, trouble him no more
Till further settling.

CORDELIA: Will't please your Highness walk?

LEAR: You must bear with me:
Pray you now forget, and forgive, I am old and foolish.

Exeunt all but Kent and Gentleman.

[GENTLEMAN: Holds it true sir, that the Duke of Cornwall was so slain?

KENT: Most certain sir.

GENTLEMAN: Who is conductor of his people?

KENT: As 'tis said, the bastard son of Gloucester.

GENTLEMAN: They say Edgar his banish'd son is with the Earl of Kent in Germany.

KENT: Report is changeable, 'tis time to look about, the powers of the kingdom approach apace.

GENTLEMAN: The arbitrement is like to be bloody, fare you well sir.

Exit.

KENT: My point and period will be throughly wrought,
Or well, or ill, as this day's battle's fought.

Exit.]

V.1

Enter with drum and colours, Bastard Regan, Gentlemen, and Soldiers.

BASTARD: Know of the Duke if his last purpose hold,
Or whether since he is advis'd by aught
To change the course; he's full of alteration,
And self-reproving; bring his constant pleasure.
REGAN: Our sister's man is certainly miscarried.
BASTARD: 'Tis to be doubted Madam.
REGAN: Now sweet Lord,
You know the goodness I intend upon you:
Tell me but truly, but then speak the truth,
Do you not love my sister?
BASTARD: In honour'd love.
REGAN: But have you never found my brother's way,
To the for-fended place?
[BASTARD: That thought abuses you.
REGAN: I am doubtful that you have been conjunct
And bosom'd with her, as far as we call hers.]
BASTARD: No by mine honour, Madam.
REGAN: I never shall endure her, dear my Lord
Be not familiar with her.
BASTARD: Fear not, she and the Duke her husband.

Enter with drum and colours, Albany, Goneril, and Soldiers.

[GONERIL: I had rather lose the battle than that sister
Should loosen him and me.]
ALBANY: Our very loving sister, well be-met:
Sir, this I heard, the King is come to his daughter
With others, whom the rigour of our state

Forc'd to cry out: [Where I could not be honest
I never yet was valiant, for this business
It touches us, as France invades our land,
Not bolds the King, with others whom I fear,
Most just and heavy causes make oppose.
BASTARD: Sir you speak nobly.]
REGAN: Why is this reason'd?
GONERIL: Combine together 'gainst the enemy:
For these domestic and particular broils,
Are not the question here.
ALBANY: Let's then determine
With th' ancient of war on our proceeding.
[BASTARD: I shall attend you presently at your tent.]
REGAN: Sister you'll go with us?
GONERIL: No.
REGAN: 'Tis most convenient, pray go with us.
GONERIL: Oh ho, I know the riddle, I will go.

Exeunt both the armies.

Enter Edgar.

EDGAR: If e'er your Grace had speech with man so poor,
Hear me one word.
ALBANY: I'll overtake you, speak.
EDGAR: Before you fight the battle, ope this letter:
If you have victory, let the trumpet sound
For him that brought it: wretched though I seem,
I can produce a champion, that will prove
What is avouched there. If you miscarry,
Your business of the world hath so an end,
And machination ceases. Fortune loves you.
ALBANY: Stay till I have read the letter.
EDGAR: I was forbid it:
When time shall serve, let but the herald cry,
And I'll appear again.

Exit.

ALBANY: Why fare thee well, I will o'erlook thy paper.

Enter Bastard.

BASTARD: The enemy's in view, draw up your powers,
Here is the guess of their true strength and forces,
By diligent discovery, but your haste
Is now urg'd on you.

ALBANY: We will greet the time.

Exit.

BASTARD: To both these sisters have I sworn my love;
Each jealous of the other, as the stung
Are of the adder. Which of them shall I take?
Both? One? Or neither? Neither can be enjoy'd
If both remain alive: to take the widow,
Exasperates, makes mad her sister Goneril,
And hardly shall I carry out my side,
Her husband being alive. Now then, we'll use
His countenance for the battle, which being done,
Let her who would be rid of him, devise
His speedy taking off. As for the mercy
Which he intends to Lear and to Cordelia,
The battle done, and they within our power,
Shall never see his pardon: for my state,
Stands on me to defend, not to debate.

Exit.

V.2

Alarum within. Enter with drum and colours, Lear, Cordelia, and Soldiers over the stage, and exeunt.
Enter Edgar, and Gloucester.

EDGAR: Here father, take the shadow of this tree
For your good host: pray that the right may thrive:
If ever I return to you again,
I'll bring you comfort.

GLOUCESTER: Grace go with you sir.

Exit Edgar.

Alarum and retreat within. Enter Edgar.

EDGAR: Away old man, give me thy hand, away:
King Lear hath lost, he and his daughter ta'en;
Give me thy hand: come on.

GLOUCESTER: No farther sir, a man may rot even here.

EDGAR: What in ill thoughts again?
Men must endure
Their going hence, even as their coming hither,
Ripeness is all: come on.

GLOUCESTER: And that's true too.

Exeunt.

V.3

Enter in conquest with drum and colours, Bastard, Lear and Cordelia, as prisoners; Soldiers, Captain.

BASTARD: Some officers take them away: good guard,
Until their greater pleasures first be known
That are to censure them.

CORDELIA: We are not the first,
Who with best meaning have incurr'd the worst:
For thee oppressed King am I cast down,
Myself could else out-frown false Fortune's frown.
Shall we not see these daughters, and these sisters?

LEAR: No, no, no, no: come let's away to prison,
We two alone will sing like birds i' th' cage:
When thou dost ask me blessing, I'll kneel down
And ask of thee forgiveness: so we'll live,
And pray, and sing, and tell old tales, and laugh
At gilded butterflies; and hear (poor rogues)

Talk of Court news, and we'll talk with them too,
Who loses, and who wins; who's in, who's out;
And take upon's the mystery of things,
As if we were God's spies: and we'll wear out
In a wall'd prison, packs and sects of great ones,
That ebb and flow by th' moon.

BASTARD: Take them away.

LEAR: Upon such sacrifices, my Cordelia,
The Gods themselves throw incense. Have I caught thee?
He that parts us, shall bring a brand from Heaven,
And fire us hence, like foxes: wipe thine eyes,
The good-years shall devour them, flesh and fell,
Ere they shall make us weep:
We'll see 'em starve first: come.

Exeunt Lear and Cordelia, guarded.

BASTARD: Come hither Captain, hark.
Take thou this note, go follow them to prison,
One step I have advanc'd thee, if thou dost
As this instructs thee, thou dost make thy way
To noble fortunes: know thou this, that men
Are as the time is; to be tender-minded
Does not become a sword, thy great employment
Will not bear question; either say thou'lt do't,
Or thrive by other means.

CAPTAIN: I'll do't, my Lord.

BASTARD: About it, and write happy, when th' hast done;
Mark I say instantly, and carry it so
As I have set it down.

[CAPTAIN: I cannot draw a cart, nor eat dried oats,
If it be man's work I'll do it.]

Exit.

Flourish. Enter Albany, Goneril, Regan, and Soldiers.

ALBANY: Sir, you have show'd to-day your valiant strain
And fortune led you well: you have the captives
Who were the opposites of this day's strife:
I do require them of you so to use them,

As we shall find their merits, and our safety
May equally determine.
BASTARD: Sir, I thought it fit,
To send the old and miserable King to some retention:
Whose age has charms in it, whose title more,
To pluck the common bosom on his side,
And turn our impress'd lances in our eyes
Which do command them. With him I sent the Queen:
My reason all the same, and they are ready
To-morrow, or at further space, t' appear
Where you shall hold your session [at this time,
We sweat and bleed, the friend hath lost his friend,
And the best quarrels in the heat are curs'd,
By those that feel their sharpness;
The question of Cordelia and her father
Requires a fitter place.]
ALBANY: Sir, by your patience,
I hold you but a subject of this war,
Not as a brother.
REGAN: That's as we list to grace him.
Methinks our pleasure might have been demanded
Ere you had spoke so far. He led our powers,
Bore the commission of my place and person,
The which immediacy may well stand up,
And call itself your brother.
GONERIL: Not so hot:
In his own grace he doth exalt himself,
More than in your addition.
REGAN: In my rights,
By me invested, he compeers the best.
GONERIL: That were the most, if he should husband you.
REGAN: Jesters do oft prove prophets.
GONERIL: Hola, hola,
That eye that told you so, look'd but a-squint.
REGAN: Lady I am not well; else I should answer
From a full-flowing stomach. General,

Take thou my soldiers, prisoners, patrimony,
Dispose of them, of me, the walls is thine:
Witness the world, that I create thee here
My Lord, and master.
GONERIL: Mean you to enjoy him?
ALBANY: The let-alone lies not in your good will.
BASTARD: Nor in thine, Lord.
ALBANY: Half-blooded fellow, yes.
REGAN: Let the drum strike, and prove my title thine.
ALBANY: Stay yet, hear reason: Edmund, I arrest thee
On capital treason; and in thy arrest,
This gilded serpent; for your claim, fair sister,
I bar it in the interest of my wife,
'Tis she is sub-contracted to this Lord,
And I her husband contradict your banns.
If you will marry, make your loves to me,
My Lady is bespoke.
GONERIL: An interlude.
ALBANY: Thou art arm'd Gloucester, let the trumpet sound:
If none appear to prove upon thy person,
Thy heinous, manifest, and many treasons,
There is my pledge: I'll make it on thy heart
Ere I taste bread, thou art in nothing less
Than I have here proclaim'd thee.
REGAN: Sick, O sick.
GONERIL: If not, I'll ne'er trust medicine.
BASTARD: There's my exchange, what in the world he is
That names me traitor, villain-like he lies,
Call by the trumpet: he that dares approach;
On him, on you, who not, I will maintain
My truth and honour firmly.

Enter a herald.

ALBANY: A herald, ho.
BASTARD: [A herald, ho, a herald.]
ALBANY: Trust to thy single virtue, for thy soldiers
All levied in my name, have in my name

Took their discharge.

REGAN: My sickness grows upon me.

ALBANY: She is not well, convey her to my tent.

Exit Regan, led.

Come hither herald, let the trumpet sound,
And read out this.

A trumpet sounds.

Herald reads.

If any man of quality or degree, within the lists of the army, will maintain upon Edmund, supposed Earl of Gloucester, that he is a manifold traitor, let him appear by the third sound of the Trumpet: he is bold in his defence.

BASTARD: Sound.

First trumpet.

HERALD: Again.

Second trumpet.

HERALD: Again.

Third trumpet.

Trumpet answers within.

Enter Edgar, at the third sound, armed, with a trumpet before him.

ALBANY: Ask him his purposes, why he appears
Upon this call o' th' trumpet.

HERALD: What are you?
Your name, your quality, and why you answer
This present summons?

EDGAR: Know my name is lost;
By treason's tooth: bare-gnawn, and canker-bit;
Yet am I noble as the adversary
I come to cope.

ALBANY: Which is that adversary?

EDGAR: What's he that speaks for Edmund Earl of Gloucester?

BASTARD: Himself, what say'st thou to him?

EDGAR: Draw thy sword,
That if my speech offend a noble heart,
Thy arm may do thee justice, here is mine:

Behold it is my privilege,
The privilege of mine honour,
My oath, and my profession. I protest,
Maugre thy strength, place, youth, and eminence,
Despite thy victor-sword, and fire-new Fortune,
Thy valour, and thy heart, thou art a traitor:
False to thy Gods, thy brother, and thy father,
Conspirant 'gainst this high-illustrious Prince,
And from th' extremest upward of thy head,
To the descent and dust below thy foot,
A most toad-spotted traitor. Say thou no,
This sword, this arm, and my best spirits are bent
To prove upon thy heart, whereto I speak,
Thou liest.

BASTARD: In wisdom I should ask thy name,
But since thy outside looks so fair and warlike,
And that thy tongue (some say) of breeding breathes,
What safe, and nicely I might well delay,
By rule of knighthood, I disdain and spurn:
Back do I toss these treasons to thy head,
With the hell-hated lie o'erwhelm thy heart,
Which for they yet glance by, and scarcely bruise,
This sword of mine shall give them instant way,
Where they shall rest for ever. Trumpets speak.

Alarums. They fight. Bastard falls.

ALBANY: Save him, save him.

GONERIL: This is practice Gloucester,
By th' Law of War, thou wast not bound to answer
An unknown opposite; thou art not vanquish'd,
But cozen'd and beguil'd.

ALBANY: Shut your mouth Dame,
Or with this paper shall I stop it: hold, sir,
Thou worse than any name, read thine own evil:
No tearing Lady, I perceive you know it.

GONERIL: Say if I do, the Laws are mine not thine,
Who can arraign me for't?

Exit.

ALBANY: Most monstrous! O, know'st thou this paper?
BASTARD: Ask me not what I know.
ALBANY: Go after her, she's desperate, govern her.
BASTARD: What you have charg'd me with, that have I done,
And more, much more, the time will bring it out.
'Tis past, and so am I: but what art thou
That hast this fortune on me? If thou'rt noble,
I do forgive thee.
EDGAR: Let's exchange charity:
I am no less in blood than thou art Edmund,
If more, the more th' hast wrong'd me.
My name is Edgar and thy father's son,
The Gods are just, and of our pleasant vices
Make instruments to plague us:
The dark and vicious place where thee he got,
Cost him his eyes.
BASTARD: Th' hast spoken right, 'tis true,
The wheel is come full circle, I am here.
ALBANY: Methought thy very gait did prophesy
A royal nobleness: I must embrace thee,
Let sorrow split my heart, if ever I
Did hate thee, or thy father.
EDGAR: Worthy Prince, I know't.
ALBANY: Where have you hid yourself?
How have you known the miseries of your father?
EDGAR: By nursing them my Lord. List a brief tale,
And when 'tis told, O that my heart would burst.
The bloody proclamation to escape
That follow'd me so near, (O our lives' sweetness,
That we the pain of death would hourly die,
Rather than die at once) taught me to shift
Into a madman's rags, t' assume a semblance
That very dogs disdain'd: and in this habit
Met I my father with his bleeding rings,
Their precious stones new lost: became his guide,

Led him, begg'd for him, sav'd him from despair.
Never (O fault) reveal'd myself unto him,
Until some half-hour past when I was arm'd,
Not sure, though hoping of this good success,
I ask'd his blessing, and from first to last
Told him our pilgrimage. But his flaw'd heart
(Alack too weak the conflict to support)
'Twixt two extremes of passion, joy and grief,
Burst smilingly.

BASTARD: This speech of yours hath mov'd me,
And shall perchance do good, but speak you on,
You look as you had something more to say.

ALBANY: If there be more, more woeful, hold it in,
For I am almost ready to dissolve,
Hearing of this.

[EDGAR: This would have seem'd a period
To such as love not sorrow, but another
To amplify too much, would make much more,
And top extremity.
Whilst I was big in clamour, came there in a man,
Who having seen me in my worst estate,
Shunn'd my abhorr'd society, but then finding
Who 'twas that so endure'd, with his strong arms
He fasten'd on my neck and bellow'd out,
As he'ld burst heaven, threw him on my father,
Told the most piteous tale of Lear and him,
That ever ear receiv'd, which in recounting
His grief grew puissant and the strings of life,
Began to crack, twice then the trumpets sounded,
And there I left him tranc'd.

ALBANY: But who was this?

EDGAR: Kent sir, the banish'd Kent, who in disguise,
Follow'd his enemy king and did him service
Improper for a slave.]

Enter a Gentleman, with a bloody knife.

GENTLEMAN: Help, help: O help.

EDGAR: What kind of help?
ALBANY: Speak man.
EDGAR: What means that bloody knife?
GENTLEMAN: 'Tis hot, it smokes, It came even from the heart of—O she's dead.
ALBANY: Who dead? Speak man.
GENTLEMAN: Your Lady sir, your Lady; and her sister
By her is poison'd: she confesses it.
BASTARD: I was contracted to them both, all three
Now marry in an instant.
EDGAR: Here comes Kent.

Enter Kent.

ALBANY: Produce the bodies, be they alive or dead;
This judgement of the Heavens that makes us tremble,
Touches us not with pity.
O, is this he?
The time will not allow the compliment
Which very manners urges.
KENT: I am come
To bid my King and master aye good night.
Is he not here?
ALBANY: Great thing of us forgot,
Speak Edmund, where's the King? and where's Cordelia?
See'st thou this object Kent?

The bodies of Goneril and Regan are brought in.

KENT: Alack, why thus?
BASTARD: Yet Edmund was belov'd:
The one the other poison'd for my sake,
And after slew herself.
ALBANY: Even so: cover their faces.
BASTARD: I pant for life: some good I mean to do
Despite of mine own Nature. Quickly send,
(Be brief in it) to th' Castle, for my writ
Is on the life of Lear and on Cordelia:
Nay, send in time.
ALBANY: Run, run, O run.

EDGAR: To who my Lord? Who has the office? send
Thy token of reprieve.
BASTARD: Well thought on, take my sword,
Give it the captain.
ALBANY: Haste thee for thy life.

Exit Gentleman.

BASTARD: He hath commission from thy wife and me,
To hang Cordelia in the prison, and
To lay the blame upon her own despair,
That she fordid herself.
ALBANY: The Gods defend her, bear him hence awhile.

Edmund is borne off.

Enter Lear with Cordelia in his arms.

LEAR: Howl, howl, howl: O you are men of stones,
Had I your tongues and eyes, I'ld use them so,
That Heaven's vault should crack: she's gone for ever.
I know when one is dead, and when one lives,
She's dead as earth: lend me a looking-glass,
If that her breath will mist or stain the stone,
Why then she lives.
KENT: Is this the promis'd end?
EDGAR: Or image of that horror?
ALBANY: Fall and cease.
LEAR: This feather stirs, she lives: if it be so,
It is a chance which does redeem all sorrows
That ever I have felt.
KENT: O my good master.
LEAR: Prithee away.
EDGAR: 'Tis noble Kent, your friend.
LEAR: A plague upon you murderers, traitors all,
I might have sav'd her, now she's gone for ever:
Cordelia, Cordelia, stay a little. Ha:
What is't thou say'st? Her voice was ever soft,
Gentle, and low, an excellent thing in woman.
I kill'd the slave that was a-hanging thee.
CAPTAIN: 'Tis true, my Lords, he did.

LEAR: Did I not fellow?
I have seen the day, with my good biting falchion
I would have made him skip: I am old now,
And these same crosses spoil me. Who are you?
Mine eyes are not o' th' best, I'll tell you straight.
KENT: If Fortune brag of two, she lov'd and hated,
One of them we behold.
LEAR: This is a dull sight, are you not Kent?
KENT: The same:
Your servant Kent, where is your servant Caius.
LEAR: He's a good fellow, I can tell you that,
He'll strike and quickly too, he's dead and rotten.
KENT: No my good Lord, I am the very man.
LEAR: I'll see that straight.
KENT: That from your first of difference and decay,
Have follow'd your sad steps.
LEAR: You are welcome hither.
KENT: Nor no man else: all's cheerless, dark, and deadly,
Your eldest daughters have fordone themselves,
And desperately are dead.
LEAR: Ay so I think.
ALBANY: He knows not what he says, and vain is it
That we present us to him.
EDGAR: Very bootless.

Enter a Messenger.

MESSENGER: Edmund is dead my Lord.
ALBANY: That's but a trifle here:
You Lords and noble friends, know our intent,
What comfort to this great decay may come,
Shall be appli'd. For us we will resign,
During the life of this old Majesty
To him our absolute power, you to your rights,
With boot, and such addition as your honours
Have more than merited. All friends shall taste
The wages of their virtue, and all foes
The cup of their deservings: O see, see.

LEAR: And my poor fool is hang'd: No, no, no life?
Why should a dog, a horse, a rat have life,
And thou no breath at all? Thou'lt come no more,
Never, never, never, never, never.
Pray you undo this button. Thank you sir.
Do you see this? Look on her? look her lips,
Look there, look there.

He dies.

EDGAR: He faints, my Lord, my Lord.
KENT: Break heart, I prithee break.
EDGAR: Look up my Lord.
KENT: Vex not his ghost, O let him pass, he hates him,
That would upon the rack of this tough world
Stretch him out longer.
EDGAR: He is gone indeed.
KENT: The wonder is, he hath endur'd so long,
He but usurp'd his life.
ALBANY: Bear them from hence, our present business
Is general woe: friends of my soul, you twain,
Rule in this Realm, and the gor'd state sustain.
KENT: I have a journey sir, shortly to go,
My master calls me, I must not say no.
ENDGAR: The weight of this sad time we must obey,
Speak what we feel, not what we ought to say:
The oldest hath borne most, we that are young,
Shall never see so much, nor live so long.

Exeunt with a dead march.

GLOSSARY

addition: title, honour.
admiration: affected wonder.
affected: shown affection for.
all-licensed: allowed to say anything.
alteration: vacillation.
anatomise: dissect.
ancient of war: experienced in war.
apish: imitative.
approves: confirms.
arbitrement: decision.
arch: chief support.
aroint: be off.
attaint: impeachment.
avert: turn.

ballow: cudgel.
bans: curses.
beguile: cheat.
bench: sit.
benison: blessing.
bewray: betray.
bias of nature: nature inclination.
biding: resting place.
blanket: cover with a blanket.
blown: puffed out.
bond: agreement, duty.
boot: advantage.
bourn: boundary.
brach: bitch.
brazed: become brazen.
breed occasions: find excuses.

cadent: falling.
canker-bit: corrupted by maggots.
carbonado: piece of meat, slashed for grilling.
carry it so: make it so appear.
casement: window.
century: company, a hundred men.
champains riched: enriched by fertile fields.
character: handwriting.
charge: expense.
choler: wrath.
chough: jackdaw.
clotpoll: blockhead.
cock: cock-boat, the ship's boat which was towed behind.
common bosom: the sympathy of the common people.
compact: made firmer, in league with.
compeers: takes equal rank.
conceit: imagination.
conjunct: allied.
constant: firm.
contemn: despise.
corky: dry, withered.
costard: lit. apple, head.

cowish: cowardly.
cozen'd: cheated.
crab: crab apple.
cross lightning: forked lightning.
crosses: troubles.
cub-drawn: sucked dry, and so hungry and ferocious.
cullionly: rascally.
curiosity: 1. niceness; 2. exactness.
curst: sharp, bitter.

dear: important.
debosh'd: debauched.
defuse: make indistinct.
depositories: trustees.
derogate: debased.
difference: quarrel.
disnature'd: unnatural.
distract: mad.
ditch-dog: dog drowned in a ditch.
doubted: feared.

ear-kissing: whispered close.
elf: tangle.
epicurism: self-indulgence.
evasion: excuse.
even o'er: go over.
eyeless: blind.

faint neglect: suspicion of neglect.
fastened: hardened.
fear judgment: respect the law.
fell: fierce.
festinate: speedy.
fetches: excuses.
flaws: pieces.
fleshment: excitement.
foins: fencing thrusts.
fond: foolish.
footed: on the move.
fordid: destroyed.
fore-vouch'd: previously declared.
for-fended: forbidden.
fork: two-pointed arrow.
fraught: laden, endowed.
fret: wear away.
frontlet: forehead, frown.
furnishings: outward trappings.

gallow: terrify.
gasted: frightened.
generous: noble.
germens: seeds of life.
glass eyes: spectacles.
goest: i.e., on foot.
got: begot.
graced: gracious, honourable.

half-blooded: bastard.
hatch: half door.
head-lugged: born by dogs in baiting.
Hecate: goddess of night and witchcraft.
high-engendered: joined on high, in the sky.
hospitable favours: features of your host.

images: signs.
impatience: suffering.
important: importunate.
impress'd lances: conscript soldiers.
ingenious: sensitive.
intelligent party: intelligence agent.
interess'd: interested.
invention: plan.
it: its.

jakes: latrine.

kibes: blisters.
knapp'd: cracked.

latch'd: wounded.
lag: lagging behind, i.e., younger.
lethargied: paralyzed.
luxury: lust.
lym: bloodhound.

machinations: plotting.
maugre: in spite of.
meads: pasture lands.
meiny: company.
minikin: dainty.
mo: more.
monsters: makes monstrous.

nether stocks: stockings.
nicely: with a nice regard for formality.
nighted: darkened.
nine-fold: with nine evil spirits.
nursery: care.

œillades: loving looks.
opposite: opponent.
orbs: stars.
out-wall: outward appearance.
overture: disclosure.
owes: owns.

packs and sects: factions and parties.
pain: labour.
'parel: apparel.
pass: pass sentence.
pelting: paltry.
perdu: sentry in an exposed position.
period: end.
pieced: add to.
pight: pledged.
placket: opening in the petticoat.
plate: protect.
poise: weight.
power: army.
practice: plot.
prefer: promote.
pregnant: able to conceive.
presently: immediately.
pressed: immediate.
prevented: forestalled.
proof and preachment: example.
propinquity: relationship.
put it on: encourage.

qualified: mixed, moderate.
question: come to life.
questrists: searchers.
quit: requite, defend.

razed: erased, disguised.
remember'st: remindest.
remorse: pity.
repeal: recall from banishment.
respect: regard for.
reverb: echo.

sallets: salads.
saw: proverb.
scanted: curtailed.
scattered: disunited.
seconds: supports.
sectary astronomical: follower of the sect of astronomers.
seeming: hypocrisy.
sequent: subsequent.
several: separate.
shealed peascod: pod without the peas.
simples operative: effective remedies.
simular: pretended.
smilets: little smiles.
snuffs and packings: offences and plots.
sovereign: ruling, predominant.
spleen: malice.
star-blasting: evil caused by the stars.
stelled fires: light of the stars.
still: always.
still-soliciting: always asking for something.
stomach: anger.
strained: excessive.
strangered: made a stranger.
sub-contracted: already bespoke.
subscription: allegiance.
sumpter: baggage animal.
superfluous: having too much.

tax: censure.
teem: breed.
temper: mix.
temperance: sanity.
tender: offer.
tender-hefted: delicately-framed.
thought-executing: killing as quick as thought.
top: head.
trowest: knowest.
trundle-tail: curly tail.

unbolted: unsifted.
undistinguished: limitless.

vent: utter.

wakes: merry makings.
wants: lacks.
washed: weeping.
web and pin: eye diseases.
weeds: garments.

well-favoured: sleek.
white herring: pickled herring.
wide-skirted: extensive.
will: 1. intention; 2. purpose; 3. lust.
wind me: insinuate.
worth: worthy.